deas expressed in this book (but not Scripture verses) are not, in all cases, exact quotations,
been edited for clarity and brevity. In all cases, the author has attempted to maintain the
ginal intent. In some cases, quoted material for this book was obtained from secondary
arily print media. While every effort was made to ensure the accuracy of these sources, the
nnot be guaranteed. For additions, deletions, corrections, or clarifications in future editions
please write Freeman-Smith.

Design by Scott Williams/Richmond & Williams
ayout by Bart Dawson

978-1-60587-384-8

Printed in China

1 2 3 4 5—RRD—16 15 14 13 12

TO

FROM

DATE:

PROMISES
From God's Word
For

MEN

INTRODUCTION

God's promises are eternal and unchanging. But, as every man knows, life in today's fast-paced world can be so demanding and so confusing that it becomes easy to forget God's blessings and His mercy. This book invites you to slow down and remind yourself of the joys and abundance that God offers to all His children, including you.

How desperately our world needs Christian men who are willing to honor God with their service. This generation faces problems that defy easy solutions, yet face them we must. We need leaders whose vision is clear and whose intentions are pure. Daniel writes, "Those who are wise will shine like the brightness of the heavens, and those who lead many to righteousness, like the stars for ever and ever" (12:3 NIV). Hopefully, you are determined to be such a man—a courageous man who offers counsel and direction to his family, to his friends, and to his coworkers.

In your hands, you hold a book that contains 40 devotional readings. Each chapter contains

Bible verses, a brief essay, inspirational quotations, and a prayer for your journey. During the next 40 days, please try this experiment: read a chapter each day. If you're already committed to a daily time of worship, this book will enrich that experience. If you are not, the simple act of giving God a few minutes each morning will change the direction and the quality of your life.

CHAPTER 1

THE PROMISE

God will never leave your side,
not even for an instant.

*The Lord is the One who will go before you.
He will be with you; He will not leave you or
forsake you. Do not be afraid or discouraged.*

—

Deuteronomy 31:8 HCSB

LIVING COURAGEOUSLY

Christians have every reason to live courageously. After all, the ultimate battle has already been fought and won on the cross at Calvary. But, even dedicated followers of Christ may find their courage tested by the inevitable disappointments and tragedies that occur in the lives of believers and non-believers alike.

Every human life is a tapestry of events: some wonderful, some not-so-wonderful, and some downright disheartening. When the storm clouds form overhead and we find ourselves wandering through the dark valley of despair, our faith is stretched, sometimes to the breaking point. But, as believers, we can be comforted: wherever we find ourselves, whether at the top of the mountain or the depths of the valley, God is there, and because He cares for us, we can live courageously.

The next time you find yourself in a fear-provoking situation, remember that God is as near as your next breath, and remember that He offers salvation to His children. He is your shield and your strength; He is your protector and your deliverer. Call upon Him in your hour of need and then be comforted. Whatever your challenge, whatever your trouble, God can handle it. And will.

PROMISES FROM GOD'S WORD

Be alert, stand firm in the faith, be brave and strong.

1 Corinthians 16:13 HCSB

For God has not given us a spirit of fearfulness, but one of power, love, and sound judgment.

2 Timothy 1:7 HCSB

Haven't I commanded you: be strong and courageous? Do not be afraid or discouraged, for the Lord your God is with you wherever you go.

Joshua 1:9 HCSB

But when Jesus heard it, He answered him, "Don't be afraid. Only believe."

Luke 8:50 HCSB

A TIMELY TIP

If you trust God completely and without reservation, you have every reason on earth—and in heaven—to live courageously. And that's precisely what you should do.

There comes a time when we simply have to face the challenges in our lives and stop backing down.

John Eldredge

Why rely on yourself and fall? Cast yourself upon His arm. Be not afraid. He will not let you slip. Cast yourself in confidence. He will receive you and heal you.

St. Augustine

Jesus Christ can make the weakest man into a divine dreadnought, fearing nothing.

Oswald Chambers

Take courage. We walk in the wilderness today and in the Promised Land tomorrow.

D. L. Moody

Do not let Satan deceive you into being afraid of God's plans for your life.

R. A. Torrey

Are you fearful? First, bow your head and pray for God's strength. Then, raise your head knowing that, together, you and God can handle whatever comes your way.

Jim Gallery

A PRAYER FOR TODAY

Dear Lord, fill me with Your Spirit and help me face my challenges with courage and determination. Keep me mindful, Father, that You are with me always—and with You by my side, I have nothing to fear. Amen

CHAPTER 2

THE PROMISE

Prayer is a powerful force,
a force that can transform your life.

The intense prayer of the righteous is very powerful.

—

James 5:16 HCSB

THE POWER OF PRAYER

The power of prayer": these words are so familiar, yet sometimes we forget what they mean. Prayer is a powerful tool for communicating with our Creator; it is an opportunity to commune with the Giver of all things good. Prayer is not a thing to be taken lightly or to be used infrequently.

All too often, amid the rush of daily life, we may lose sight of God's presence in our lives. Instead of turning to Him for guidance and for comfort, we depend, instead, upon our own resources. To do so is a profound mistake. Prayer should never be reserved for mealtimes or for bedtimes; it should be an ever-present focus in our daily lives.

In his first letter to the Thessalonians, Paul wrote, "Rejoice evermore. Pray without ceasing. In every thing give thanks: for this is the will of God in Christ Jesus concerning you" (5:17-18 KJV). Paul's words apply to every Christian of every generation.

Today, instead of turning things over in our minds, let us turn them over to God in prayer.

Instead of worrying about our decisions, let's trust God to help us make them. Today, let us pray constantly about things great and small. God is listening, and He wants to hear from us. Now.

PROMISES FROM GOD'S WORD

Let the words of my mouth and the meditation of my heart be acceptable in Your sight, O Lord, my strength and my Redeemer.

Psalm 19:14 NKJV

Rejoice in hope; be patient in affliction; be persistent in prayer.

Romans 12:12 HCSB

Yet He often withdrew to deserted places and prayed.

Luke 5:16 HCSB

The Lord is far from the wicked but he hears the prayer of the righteous.

Proverbs 15:29 NIV

A TIMELY TIP

Prayer changes things and it changes you. So pray.

—————

Obedience is the master key to effective prayer.

Billy Graham

Prayer may not get us what we want, but it will teach us to want what we need.

Vance Havner

It is well said that neglected prayer is the birth-place of all evil.

C. H. Spurgeon

Those who know God the best are the richest and most powerful in prayer. Little acquaintance with God, and strangeness and coldness to Him, make prayer a rare and feeble thing.

E. M. Bounds

Learn to pray to God in such a way that you are trusting Him as your Physician to do what He knows is best. Confess to Him the disease, and let Him choose the remedy.

St. Augustine

Pour out your heart to God and tell Him how you feel. Be real, be honest, and when you get it all out, you'll start to feel the gradual covering of God's comforting presence.

Bill Hybels

A PRAYER FOR TODAY

Dear Lord, make me a man of constant prayer. Your Holy Word commands me to pray without ceasing. Let me take everything to You. When I am discouraged, let me pray. When I am lonely, let me take my sorrows to You. And when I am joyful, let me offer up prayers of thanksgiving. In all things great and small, at all times, whether happy or sad, let me seek Your wisdom and Your Grace . . . in prayer. Amen

CHAPTER 3

THE PROMISE

God's Word is a perfect prescription
for every aspect of your life.

*All Scripture is inspired by God and is profitable
for teaching, for rebuking, for correcting,
for training in righteousness,
so that the man of God may be complete,
equipped for every good work.*

—

2 Timothy 3:16-17 HCSB

TRUSTING GOD'S PROMISES

God's promises are found in a book like no other: the Holy Bible. The Bible is a road map for life here on earth and for life eternal. As Christians, we are called upon to trust its promises, to follow its commandments, and to share its Good News.

As believers, we must study the Bible daily and meditate upon its meaning for our lives. Otherwise, we deprive ourselves of a priceless gift from our Creator. God's Holy Word is, indeed, a transforming, life-changing, one-of-a-kind treasure. And, a passing acquaintance with the Good Book is insufficient for Christians who seek to obey God's Word and to understand His will.

God has made promises to mankind and to you. God's promises never fail and they never grow old. You must trust those promises and share them with your family, with your friends, and with the world.

PROMISES FROM GOD'S WORD

Man shall not live by bread alone, but by every word that proceeds from the mouth of God.

Matthew 4:4 NKJV

For I am not ashamed of the gospel, because it is God's power for salvation to everyone who believes.

Romans 1:16 HCSB

Heaven and earth will pass away, but My words will never pass away.

Matthew 24:35 HCSB

For the word of God is living and effective and sharper than any two-edged sword, penetrating as far as to divide soul, spirit, joints, and marrow; it is a judge of the ideas and thoughts of the heart.

Hebrews 4:12 HCSB

A TIMELY TIP

Charles Swindoll writes, "There are four words I wish we would never forget, and they are, 'God keeps his word.'" And, when it comes to studying God's Word, school is always in session.

Nobody ever outgrows Scripture; the book widens and deepens with our years.

C. H. Spurgeon

Faith is the virtue that enables us to believe and obey the Word of God, for faith comes from hearing and hearing from the Word of God.

Franklin Graham

Meditating upon His Word will inevitably bring peace of mind, strength of purpose, and power for living.

Bill Bright

When you meet with God, open the Bible. Don't rely on your memory; rely on those printed pages.

Charles Swindoll

Cling to the whole Bible, not to part of it. A man is not going to do much with a broken sword.

D. L. Moody

It takes calm, thoughtful, prayerful meditation on the Word to extract its deepest nourishment.

Vance Havner

A PRAYER FOR TODAY

Heavenly Father, Your Holy Word is a light unto the world; let me study it, trust it, and share it with all who cross my path. In all that I do, help me be a worthy witness for You as I share the Good News of Your perfect Son and Your perfect Word. Amen

CHAPTER 4

THE PROMISE

Because God will care for you now
and forever, you need not worry.

*So don't worry, saying, "What will we eat?" or
"What will we drink?" or "What will we wear?"
For the Gentiles eagerly seek all these things,
and your heavenly Father knows that you need
them. But seek first the kingdom of God and His
righteousness, and all these things will be provided
for you. Therefore don't worry about tomorrow,
because tomorrow will worry about itself.
Each day has enough trouble of its own.*

—

Matthew 6:31-34 HCSB

BEYOND WORRY

If you are a man with lots of obligations and plenty of responsibilities, it is simply a fact of life: you worry. From time to time, you worry about health, about finances, about safety, about family, and about countless other concerns, some great and some small.

Where is the best place to take your worries? Take them to God. Take your troubles to Him; take your fears to Him; take your doubts to Him; take your weaknesses to Him; take your sorrows to Him . . . and leave them all there. Seek protection from the One who offers you eternal salvation; build your spiritual house upon the Rock that cannot be moved.

Perhaps you are uncertain about your future or your finances—or perhaps you are simply a "worrier" by nature. If so, it's time to focus less on your troubles and more on God's promises. And that's as it should be because God is trustworthy . . . and you are protected.

PROMISES FROM GOD'S WORD

Your heart must not be troubled. Believe in God; believe also in Me.

John 14:1 HCSB

Come to Me, all you who labor and are heavy laden, and I will give you rest. Take My yoke upon you and learn from Me, for I am gentle and lowly in heart, and you will find rest for your souls. For My yoke is easy and My burden is light.

Matthew 11:28-30 NKJV

I will be with you when you pass through the waters . . . when you walk through the fire . . . the flame will not burn you. For I the Lord your God, the Holy One of Israel, and your Savior.

Isaiah 43:2-3 HCSB

Don't worry about anything, but in everything, through prayer and petition with thanksgiving, let your requests be made known to God.

Philippians 4:6 HCSB

A TIMELY TIP

An important part of becoming a more mature Christian is learning to worry less and to trust God more.

God is bigger than your problems. Whatever worries press upon you today, put them in God's hands and leave them there.

Billy Graham

The beginning of anxiety is the end of faith, and the beginning of true faith is the end of anxiety.

George Mueller

Much that worries us beforehand can, quite unexpectedly, have a happy and simple solution. Worries just don't matter. Things really are in a better hand than ours.

Dietrich Bonhoeffer

Today is the tomorrow we worried about yesterday.

Dennis Swanberg

We know so little about the future that to worry about it would be the height of foolishness.

C. H. Spurgeon

Worry and anxiety are sand in the machinery of life; faith is the oil.

E. Stanley Jones

A PRAYER FOR TODAY

Forgive me, Lord, when I worry. Worry reflects a lack of trust in Your ability to meet my every need. Help me to work, Lord, and not to worry. And, keep me mindful, Father, that nothing, absolutely nothing, will happen this day that You and I cannot handle together. Amen

CHAPTER 5

THE PROMISE

When you become the right kind
of leader, God will give you
more responsibility.

—

*His master said to him, "Well done, good and
faithful slave! You were faithful over a few things;
I will put you in charge of many things.
Enter your master's joy!"*

—

Matthew 25:21 HCSB

THE RIGHT KIND OF LEADERSHIP

The old saying is familiar and true: imitation is the sincerest form of flattery. As believers, we are called to imitate, as best we can, Christ Jesus. The task of imitating Him is often difficult and sometimes impossible, but as Christians, we must continue to try.

Our world needs leaders who willingly honor Christ with their words and their deeds, but not necessarily in that order. If you seek to be such a leader, then you must begin by making yourself a worthy example to your family, to your friends, to your church, and to your community. After all, your words of instruction will never ring true unless you yourself are willing to follow them.

Christ-centered leadership is an exercise in service: service to God in heaven and service to His children here on earth. Christ willingly became a servant to His followers, and you must seek to do the same for yours.

Are you the kind of servant-leader whom you would want to follow? If so, congratulations: you are honoring your Savior by imitating Him. And that, of course, is the sincerest form of flattery.

PROMISES FROM GOD'S WORD

And we exhort you, brothers: warn those who are lazy, comfort the discouraged, help the weak, be patient with everyone.

1 Thessalonians 5:14 HCSB

Shepherd God's flock among you, not overseeing out of compulsion but freely, according to God's will; not for the money but eagerly.

1 Peter 5:2 HCSB

An overseer, therefore, must be above reproach, the husband of one wife, self-controlled, sensible, respectable, hospitable, an able teacher, not addicted to wine, not a bully but gentle, not quarrelsome, not greedy.

1 Timothy 3:2-3 HCSB

So then, we must pursue what promotes peace and what builds up one another.

Romans 14:19 HCSB

A TIMELY TIP

Leadership comes in many forms, and you can lead others in your own way using your own style.

⊷ ⊱⊰ ⊶

A true and safe leader is likely to be one who has not desire to lead, but is forced into a position of leadership by inward pressure of the Holy Spirit and the press of external situation.

A. W. Tozer

A man ought to live so that everybody knows he is a Christian, and most of all, his family ought to know.

D. L. Moody

Leaders must learn how to wait. Often their followers don't always see as far as they see or have the faith that they have.

Warren Wiersbe

A wise leader chooses a variety of gifted individuals. He complements his strengths.

Charles Stanley

You can never separate a leader's actions from his character.

John Maxwell

Integrity and maturity are two character traits vital to the heart of a leader.

Charles Stanley

A PRAYER FOR TODAY

Dear Lord, when I find myself in a position of leadership, let me seek Your will and obey Your commandments. Make me a man of integrity and wisdom, Lord, and make me a worthy example to those whom I serve. Let me be a Christ-centered leader, and let me turn to You, Father, for guidance, for courage, for wisdom, and for love. Amen

CHAPTER 6

THE PROMISE

God has a plan for your life,
a unique path along which
He will guide you if you let Him.

*For it is God who is working among you both
the willing and the working for His good purpose.*

—

Philippians 2:13 HCSB

FINDING PURPOSE

God has a plan for your life—a plan that is near and dear to His heart. If you genuinely seek to fulfill God's plan for your life, then you must do this: you must make decisions that are pleasing to Him. The most important decision of your life is, of course, your commitment to accept God's Son as your personal Lord and Savior. And, once your eternal destiny is secured, you will undoubtedly ask yourself the question, "What now, Lord?" If you earnestly seek God's will, you will find it . . . in time.

Life is best lived on purpose. And purpose, like everything else in the universe, begins in the heart of God. Whether you realize it or not, God has a direction for your life, a divine calling, a path along which He intends to lead you. When you welcome God into your heart and establish a genuine relationship with Him, He will begin—and He will continue—to make His purposes known.

Sometimes, God's intentions will be clear to you; other times, God's plan will seem uncertain at best. But even on those difficult days when you are unsure which way to turn, you must never lose sight of these overriding facts: God created you for a reason; He has important work for you to do; and He's waiting patiently for you to do it. So why not begin today?

PROMISES FROM GOD'S WORD

We know that all things work together for the good of those who love God: those who are called according to His purpose.

Romans 8:28 HCSB

Commit your activities to the Lord and your plans will be achieved.

Proverbs 16:3 HCSB

You reveal the path of life to me; in Your presence is abundant joy; in Your right hand are eternal pleasures.

Psalm 16:11 HCSB

A TIMELY TIP

God has a wonderful plan for your life. And the time to start looking for that plan—and living it—is now.

God wants to revolutionize our lives—by showing us how knowing Him can be the most powerful force to help us become all we want to be.

Whatever purpose motivates your life, it must be something big enough and grand enough to make the investment worthwhile.

Warren Wiersbe

God wants to revolutionize our lives—by showing us how knowing Him can be the most powerful force to help us become all we want to be.

Bill Hybels

Their distress is due entirely to their deliberate determination to use themselves for a purpose other than God's.

Oswald Chambers

Without God, life has no purpose, and without purpose, life has no meaning.

Rick Warren

Waiting means going about our assigned tasks, confident that God will provide the meaning and the conclusions.

Eugene Peterson

The worst thing that laziness does is rob a man of spiritual purpose.

Billy Graham

A PRAYER FOR TODAY

Dear Lord, I know that You have a purpose for my life, and I will seek that purpose today and every day that I live. Let my actions be pleasing to You, and let me share Your Good News with a world that so desperately needs Your healing hand and the salvation of Your Son. Amen

CHAPTER 7

THE PROMISE

When you work diligently
and enthusiastically,
your efforts will be rewarded.

He did it with all his heart. So he prospered.

—

2 Chronicles 31:21 NKJV

WORKING FOR THE LORD

The old adage is both familiar and true: we must pray as if everything depended upon God, but work as if everything depended upon us. Yet sometimes, when we are weary and discouraged, we may allow our worries to sap our energy and our hope. God has other intentions. God intends that we pray for things, and He intends that we be willing to work for the things that we pray for. More importantly, God intends that our work should become His work.

Are you willing to work diligently for yourself, for your family, and for your God? And are you willing to engage in work that is pleasing to your Creator? If so, you can expect your Heavenly Father to bring forth a rich harvest.

And if you have concerns about the inevitable challenges of everyday living, take those concerns to God in prayer. He will guide your steps, He will steady your hand, He will calm your fears, and He will reward your efforts.

PROMISES FROM GOD'S WORD

Whatever you do, do it enthusiastically, as something done for the Lord and not for men.

Colossians 3:23 HCSB

Whatever your hands find to do, do with [all] your strength.

Ecclesiastes 9:10 HCSB

Don't work only while being watched, in order to please men, but as slaves of Christ, do God's will from your heart. Render service with a good attitude, as to the Lord and not to men.

Ephesians 6:6-7 HCSB

We must do the works of Him who sent Me while it is day. Night is coming when no one can work.

John 9:4 HCSB

The people had a mind to work.

Nehemiah 4:6 KJV

A TIMELY TIP

When you find work that pleases God—and when you apply yourself conscientiously to the job at hand—you'll be rewarded.

Thank God every morning when you get up that you have something which must be done, whether you like it or not. Work breeds a hundred virtues that idleness never knows.

Charles Kingsley

It may be that the day of judgment will dawn tomorrow; in that case, we shall gladly stop working for a better tomorrow. But not before.

Dietrich Bonhoeffer

Freedom is not an absence of responsibility; but rather a reward we receive when we've performed our responsibility with excellence.

Charles Swindoll

We must trust as if it all depended on God and work as if it all depended on us.

C. H. Spurgeon

The world does not consider labor a blessing, therefore it flees and hates it, but the pious who fear the Lord labor with a ready and cheerful heart, for they know God's command, and they acknowledge His calling.

Martin Luther

Few things fire up a person's commitment like dedication to excellence.

John Maxwell

A PRAYER FOR TODAY

Dear Lord, make my work pleasing to You. Help me to sow the seeds of Your abundance everywhere I go. Let me be diligent in all my undertakings and give me patience to wait for Your harvest. Amen

CHAPTER 8

THE PROMISE

God rewards humility
and punishes pride.

You will save the humble people;
But Your eyes are on the haughty,
that You may bring them down.

—

2 Samuel 22:28 NKJV

LIVING HUMBLY

As fallible human beings, we have so much to be humble about. Why, then, is humility such a difficult trait for us to master? Yet if we are to grow and mature as Christians, we must strive to give credit where credit is due, starting, of course, with God and His only begotten Son.

As Christians, we have been refashioned and saved by Jesus Christ, and that salvation came not because of our own good works but because of God's grace. Thus, we are not "self-made"; we are "God-made" and we are "Christ-saved." How, then, can we be boastful? The answer, of course, is that, if we are honest with ourselves and with our God, we simply can't be boastful . . . we must, instead, be eternally grateful and exceedingly humble. Humility, however, is not easy for most of us. All too often, we are tempted to stick out our chests and say, "Look at me; look what I did!" But, in the quiet moments when we search the depths of our own hearts, we know better. Whatever "it" is, God did that. And He deserves the credit.

PROMISES FROM GOD'S WORD

But He said to me, "My grace is sufficient for you, for power is perfected in weakness." Therefore, I will most gladly boast all the more about my weaknesses, so that Christ's power may reside in me.

2 Corinthians 12:9 HCSB

Do nothing out of rivalry or conceit, but in humility consider others as more important than yourselves.

Philippians 2:3 HCSB

If My people who are called by My name will humble themselves, and pray and seek My face, and turn from their wicked ways, then I will hear from heaven, and will forgive their sin and heal their land.

2 Chronicles 7:14 NKJV

Humble yourselves before the Lord, and He will exalt you.

James 4:10 HCSB

A TIMELY TIP

You must remain humble or face the consequences. Pride does go before the fall, but humility often prevents the fall.

Because Christ Jesus came to the world clothed in humility, he will always be found among those who are clothed with humility. He will be found among the humble people.

A. W. Tozer

Humility is the fairest and rarest flower that blooms.

Charles Swindoll

Humility is an attitude. The Lord is high and lifted up, and we are supposed to take a position of lowliness.

Franklin Graham

We can never have more of true faith than we have of true humility.

Andrew Murray

Let the love of Christ be believed in and felt in your hearts, and it will humble you.

C. H. Spurgeon

A humble heart is like a magnet that draws the favor of God toward us.

Jim Cymbala

A PRAYER FOR TODAY

Lord, make me a man with a humble heart. Keep me mindful, Dear God, that all my gifts come from You. When I feel prideful, remind me that You sent Your Son to be a humble carpenter and that Jesus was ridiculed on a cross. Let me grow beyond my need for earthly praise, Lord, and when I seek approval, let me look only to You. Amen

CHAPTER 9

THE PROMISE

God rewards honesty,
and He punishes dishonesty.

*The man of integrity walks securely,
but he who takes crooked paths will be found out.*

—

Proverbs 10:9 NIV

THE IMPORTANCE OF CHARACTER

Charles Swindoll correctly observed, "Nothing speaks louder or more powerfully than a life of integrity." Righteous men agree.

Character is built slowly over a lifetime. It is the sum of every right decision, every honest word, every noble thought, and every heartfelt prayer. It is forged on the anvil of honorable work and polished by the twin virtues of generosity and humility. Character is a precious thing—difficult to build but easy to tear down. As believers in Christ, we must seek to live each day with discipline, honesty, and faith. When we do, integrity becomes a habit.

If you sincerely wish to be a righteous man, then you must walk with God and you must follow His commandments. When you do, your character will take care of itself . . . and God will surely smile upon you and yours.

PROMISES FROM GOD'S WORD

As the water reflects the face, so the heart reflects the person.

Proverbs 27:19 HCSB

Do not be deceived: "Evil company corrupts good habits."

1 Corinthians 15:33 NKJV

We also rejoice in our afflictions, because we know that affliction produces endurance, endurance produces proven character, and proven character produces hope.

Romans 5:3-4 HCSB

A good name is to be chosen rather than great riches, loving favor rather than silver and gold.

Proverbs 22:1 NKJV

A TIMELY TIP

Character matters. Your ability to witness for Christ depends more upon your actions than your words.

The trials of life can be God's tools for engraving His image on our character.

Warren Wiersbe

Honesty has a beautiful and refreshing simplicity about it. No ulterior motives. No hidden meanings. As honesty and integrity characterize our lives, there will be no need to manipulate others.

Charles Swindoll

The single most important element in any human relationship is honesty—with oneself, with God, and with others.

Catherine Marshall

Integrity is not a given factor in everyone's life. It is a result of self-discipline, inner trust, and a decision to be relentlessly honest in all situations in our lives.

John Maxwell

Character is both developed and revealed by tests, and all of life is a test.

Rick Warren

Character is made in the small moments of our lives.

Phillips Brooks

A PRAYER FOR TODAY

Dear Lord, make me a man whose conduct is honorable. Make me a man whose words are true. Give me the wisdom to know right from wrong, and give me the courage—and the skill—to do what needs to be done in the service of Your Son. Amen

CHAPTER 10

THE PROMISE

When we encourage each other and
share the Good News of Christ,
we are following God's will
by obeying His Word.

Carry one another's burdens;
in this way you will fulfill the law of Christ.

—

Galatians 6:2 HCSB

THE POWER OF ENCOURAGEMENT

Life is a team sport, and all of us need occasional pats on the back from our teammates. As Christians, we are called upon to spread the Good News of Christ, and we are also called to spread a message of encouragement and hope to the world.

In the Book of Ephesians, Paul writes, "Do not let any unwholesome talk come out of your mouths, but only what is helpful for building others up according to their needs, that it may benefit those who listen" (4:29 NIV). Paul reminds us that when we choose our words carefully, we can have a powerful impact on those around us.

Whether you realize it or not, many people with whom you come in contact every day are in desperate need of a smile or an encouraging word. The world can be a difficult place, and countless friends and family members may be troubled by the challenges of everyday life. Since we don't always know who needs our help, the best strategy is to encourage all the people who cross our paths. So today, be a world-class source of encouragement to everyone you meet.

PROMISES FROM GOD'S WORD

Anxiety in a man's heart weighs it down, but a good word cheers it up.

Proverbs 12:25 HCSB

I want their hearts to be encouraged and joined together in love, so that they may have all the riches of assured understanding, and have the knowledge of God's mystery—Christ.

Colossians 2:2 HCSB

But encourage each other daily, while it is still called today, so that none of you is hardened by sin's deception.

Hebrews 3:13 HCSB

And let us be concerned about one another in order to promote love and good works.

Hebrews 10:24 HCSB

Therefore encourage one another and build each other up as you are already doing.

1 Thessalonians 5:11 HCSB

A TIMELY TIP

Encouragement is contagious. You can't lift other people up without lifting yourself up, too.

＊—⊨⊩—＊

A lot of people have gone further than they thought they could because someone else thought they could.

Zig Ziglar

God grant that we may not hinder those who are battling their way slowly into the light.

Oswald Chambers

We have the Lord, but He Himself has recognized that we need the touch of a human hand. He Himself came down and lived among us as a man. We cannot see Him now, but blessed be the tie that binds human hearts in Christian love.

Vance Havner

I can usually sense that a leading is from the Holy Spirit when it calls me to humble myself, to serve somebody, to encourage somebody, or to give something away. Very rarely will the evil one lead us to do those kind of things.

Bill Hybels

The truest help we can render an afflicted man is not to take his burden from him, but to call out his best energy, that he may be able to bear the burden himself.

Phillips Brooks

A PRAYER FOR TODAY

Dear Lord, let me celebrate the accomplishments of others. Make me a source of genuine, lasting encouragement to my family and friends. And let my words and deeds be worthy of Your Son, the One who gives me strength and salvation, this day and for all eternity. Amen

CHAPTER 11

THE PROMISE

When you live in the light—
and when you set a good example
for others to follow—your actions
will be pleasing to God.

*For you were once darkness, but now you
are light in the Lord. Walk as children of light—
for the fruit of the light results in all goodness,
righteousness, and truth—discerning
what is pleasing to the Lord.*

—

Ephesians 5:8-10 HCSB

THE RIGHT KIND OF EXAMPLE

Okay, here's a question: What kind of example are you? Are you the kind of man whose life serves as a powerful example of decency and morality? Are you a man whose behavior serves as a positive role model for others? Are you the kind of man whose actions, day in and day out, are based upon integrity, fidelity, and a love for the Lord? If so, you are not only blessed by God, but you are also a powerful force for good in a world that desperately needs positive influences such as yours.

We live in a dangerous, temptation-filled world. That's why you encounter so many opportunities to stray from God's commandments. Resist those temptations! When you do, you'll earn God's blessings and you'll serve as a positive role model for your family and friends.

Phillips Brooks advised, "Be such a man, and live such a life, that if every man were such as you, and every life a life like yours, this earth would be God's Paradise." And that's sound advice because our families and friends are watching . . . and so, for that matter, is God.

PROMISES FROM GOD'S WORD

Therefore since we also have such a large cloud of witnesses surrounding us, let us lay aside every weight and the sin that so easily ensnares us, and run with endurance the race that lies before us.

Hebrews 12:1 HCSB

For the kingdom of God is not in talk but in power.

1 Corinthians 4:20 HCSB

You should be an example to the believers in speech, in conduct, in love, in faith, in purity.

1 Timothy 4:12 HCSB

Do everything without grumbling and arguing, so that you may be blameless and pure.

Philippians 2:14–15 HCSB

Set an example of good works yourself, with integrity and dignity in your teaching.

Titus 2:7 HCSB

A TIMELY TIP

Your life is a sermon. What kind of sermon will you preach? The words you choose to speak may have a significant impact on others, but not as much impact as the life you choose to live.

There is no way to grow a saint overnight. Character, like the oak tree, does not spring up like a mushroom.

Vance Havner

If we have the true love of God in our hearts, we will show it in our lives. We will not have to go up and down the earth proclaiming it. We will show it in everything we say or do.

D. L. Moody

The best evidence of our having the truth is our walking in the truth.

Matthew Henry

Integrity of heart is indispensable.

John Calvin

What we practice, not (save at rare intervals) what we preach, is usually our great contribution to the conversion of others.

C. S. Lewis

Having a doctrine pass before the mind is not what the Bible means by knowing the truth. It's only when it reaches down deep into the heart that the truth begins to set us free, just as a key must penetrate a lock to turn it, or as rainfall must saturate the earth down to the roots in order for your garden to grow.

John Eldredge

A PRAYER FOR TODAY

Dear Lord, let my light shine brightly for You. Let me be a positive example for all to see, and let me share love and kindness with my family and friends, today and every day. Amen

CHAPTER 12

THE PROMISE

God has given you special talents and
unique opportunities for a good reason:
to use them.

Do not neglect the gift that is in you.

—

1 Timothy 4:14 HCSB

USING YOUR TALENTS

God knew precisely what He was doing when He gave you a unique set of talents and opportunities. And now, God wants you to use those talents for the glory of His kingdom. So here's the $64,000 question: Are you going to use those talents, or not?

Our Heavenly Father instructs us to be faithful stewards of the gifts that He bestows upon us. But we live in a world that encourages us to do otherwise. Ours is a society that is filled to the brim with countless opportunities to squander our time, our resources, and our talents. So we must be watchful for distractions and temptations that might lead us astray.

If you're sincerely interested in building a successful career, build it upon the talents that God (in His infinite wisdom) has given you. Don't try to build a career around the talents you wish He had given you.

God has blessed you with unique opportunities to serve Him, and He has given you every tool that you need to do so. Today, accept this challenge: value the talent that God has given you, nourish it, make it grow, and share it with the world. After all, the best way to say "Thank You" for God's gifts is to use them.

PROMISES FROM GOD'S WORD

Each one has his own gift from God, one in this manner and another in that.

1 Corinthians 7:7 NKJV

I remind you to keep ablaze the gift of God that is in you.

2 Timothy 1:6 HCSB

According to the grace given to us, we have different gifts: If prophecy, use it according to the standard of faith; if service, in service; if teaching, in teaching; if exhorting, in exhortation; giving, with generosity; leading, with diligence; showing mercy, with cheerfulness.

Romans 12:6-8 HCSB

A TIMELY TIP

God has given you a unique array of talents and opportunities. The rest is up to you.

You are a unique blend of talents, skills, and gifts, which makes you an indispensable member of the body of Christ.

Charles Stanley

God has given you a unique set of talents and opportunities—talents and opportunities that can be built up or buried—and the choice to build or bury is entirely up to you.

Jim Gallery

Employ whatever God has entrusted you with, in doing good, all possible good, in every possible kind and degree.

John Wesley

If you want to reach your potential, you need to add a strong work ethic to your talent.

John Maxwell

You are the only person on earth who can use your ability.

Zig Ziglar

In the great orchestra we call life, you have an instrument and a song, and you owe it to God to play them both sublimely.

Max Lucado

A PRAYER FOR TODAY

Father, because of Your promises I can live courageously. But make me fearful of displeasing You. Let me fear complacency in doing Your kingdom's work, and make me a faithful steward of the gifts You have entrusted to me. Amen

CHAPTER 13

THE PROMISE

When you faithfully live in accordance
with the Golden Rule, you will,
in time, be blessed because of
your faithfulness.

And let us not grow weary while doing good,
for in due season we shall reap
if we do not lose heart.

—

Galatians 6:9 NKJV

THE RULE THAT'S GOLDEN

Is the Golden Rule your rule, or is it just another Bible verse that goes in one ear and out the other? Jesus made Himself perfectly clear: He instructed you to treat other people in the same way that you want to be treated. But sometimes, especially when you're feeling pressure from friends, or when you're tired or upset, obeying the Golden Rule can seem like an impossible task—but it's not.

God wants each of us to treat other people with respect, kindness, and courtesy. He wants us to rise above our own imperfections, and He wants us to treat others with unselfishness and love. To make it short and sweet, God wants us to obey the Golden Rule, and He knows we can do it.

So if you're wondering how to treat someone else, ask the person you see every time you look into the mirror. The answer you receive will tell you exactly what to do.

PROMISES FROM GOD'S WORD

Therefore, whatever you want others to do for you, do also the same for them—this is the Law and the Prophets.

Matthew 7:12 HCSB

If you really carry out the royal law prescribed in Scripture, you shall love your neighbor as yourself, you are doing well.

James 2:8 HCSB

Never walk away from someone who deserves help; your hand is God's hand for that person.

Proverbs 3:27 MSG

Be kindly affectionate to one another with brotherly love, in honor giving preference to one another; not lagging in diligence, fervent in spirit, serving the Lord; rejoicing in hope, patient in tribulation, continuing steadfastly in prayer.

Romans 12:10-12 NKJV

A TIMELY TIP

Kindness is contagious. So make sure that your family and friends—and even strangers—catch it from you!

Kindness is contagious. So make sure that your
family and friends—and even strangers—catch it
from you!

If you want to be truly happy, you won't find it on an endless quest for more stuff. You'll find it in receiving God's generosity and in passing that generosity along.

Bill Hybels

Do all the good you can. By all the means you can. In all the ways you can. In all the places you can. At all the times you can. To all the people you can. As long as ever you can.

John Wesley

We are never more like God than when we give.

Charles Swindoll

The Golden Rule starts at home, but it should never stop there.

Marie T. Freeman

Faith never asks whether good works are to be done, but has done them before there is time to ask the question, and it is always doing them.

Martin Luther

The #1 rule of friendship is the Golden one.

Jim Gallery

Abundant living means abundant giving.

E. Stanley Jones

A PRAYER FOR TODAY

Dear God, help me remember to treat other people in the same way that I would want to be treated if I were in their shoes. The Golden Rule is Your rule, Father; I'll make it my rule, too. Amen

CHAPTER 14

THE PROMISE

Faith always conquers adversity.

Whatever has been born of God conquers the world. This is the victory that has conquered the world: our faith.

—

1 John 5:4 HCSB

OVERCOMING ADVERSITY

From time to time, all of us face adversity, hardship, disappointment, and loss. Old Man Trouble pays periodic visits to each of us; none of us is exempt. When we are troubled, God stands ready and willing to protect us. Our responsibility, of course, is to ask Him for protection. When we call upon Him in heartfelt prayer, He will answer—in His own time and in accordance with His own perfect plan.

Our world continues to change, but God's love remains constant. And, He remains ready to comfort us and strengthen us whenever we turn to Him. Psalm 145 promises, "The Lord is near to all who call on him, to all who call on him in truth. He fulfills the desires of those who fear him; he hears their cry and saves them" (vv. 18-20 NIV).

Life is often challenging, but as Christians, we must not be afraid. God loves us, and He will protect us. In times of hardship, He will comfort us; in times of sorrow, He will dry our tears. When we are troubled, or weak, or sorrowful, God is always with us. We must build our lives on the Rock that cannot be shaken . . . we must trust in God. Always.

PROMISES FROM GOD'S WORD

I called to the Lord in my distress; I called to my God. From His temple He heard my voice.

2 Samuel 22:7 HCSB

Consider it a great joy, my brothers, whenever you experience various trials, knowing that the testing of your faith produces endurance. But endurance must do its complete work, so that you may be mature and complete, lacking nothing.

James 1:2-4 HCSB

When you are in distress and all these things have happened to you, you will return to the Lord your God in later days and obey Him. He will not leave you, destroy you, or forget the covenant with your fathers that He swore to them by oath, because the Lord your God is a compassionate God.

Deuteronomy 4:30-31 HCSB

A TIMELY TIP

When tough times arrive, you should work as if everything depended on you and pray as if everything depended on God.

The sermon of your life in tough times ministers to people more powerfully than the most eloquent speaker.

Bill Bright

The only way to learn a strong faith is to endure great trials. I have learned my faith by standing firm amid the most severe of tests.

George Mueller

If you learn to trust God with a child-like dependence on Him as your loving heavenly Father, no trouble can destroy you.

Billy Graham

As sure as God puts his children in the furnace, he will be in the furnace with them.

C. H. Spurgeon

Throughout history, when God's people found themselves facing impossible odds, they reminded themselves of God's limitless power.

Bill Hybels

A PRAYER FOR TODAY

Dear Heavenly Father, You are my strength and my protector. When I am troubled, You comfort me. When I am discouraged, You lift me up. When I am afraid, You deliver me. Let me turn to You, Lord, when I am weak. In times of adversity, let me trust Your plan and Your will for my life. Your love is infinite, as is Your wisdom. Whatever my circumstances, Dear Lord, let me always give the praise, and the thanks, and the glory to You. Amen

CHAPTER 15

THE PROMISE

When you seek God's will
and obey His commandments,
you will be blessed.

*Whoever does the will of God
is My brother and sister and mother.*

—

Mark 3:35 HCSB

TRUSTING GOD'S WILL

When Jesus confronted the reality of His impending death on the cross, He asked God that this terrible burden might be lifted. But as He faced the possibility of a suffering that was beyond description, Jesus prayed, "Nevertheless not my will, but thine, be done" (Luke 22:42 KJV). As Christians, we too must be willing to accept God's will, even when we do not fully understand the reasons for the hardships that we must endure.

When we lose a loved one, or when we experience any other profound loss, darkness overwhelms us for a while, and it seems as if we cannot summon the strength to face another day—but, with God's help, we can. When we confront circumstances that trouble us to the very core of our souls, we must trust God. When we are worried, we must turn our concerns over to Him. When we are anxious, we must be still and listen for the quiet assurance of God's promises. And then, by placing our lives in His hands, we learn that He is our Shepherd today and throughout eternity. Let us trust the Shepherd.

PROMISES FROM GOD'S WORD

For this is the love of God, that we keep His commandments. And His commandments are not burdensome.

1 John 5:3 NKJV

Commit your activities to the Lord and your plans will be achieved.

Proverbs 16:3 HCSB

Father, if You are willing, take this cup away from Me—nevertheless, not My will, but Yours, be done.

Luke 22:42 HCSB

And do not be conformed to this world, but be transformed by the renewing of your mind, that you may prove what is that good and acceptable and perfect will of God.

Romans 12:2 NKJV

A TIMELY TIP

When God's will becomes your will, good things happen.

Our Lord never asks us to decide for Him; He asks us to yield to Him—a very different matter.

Oswald Chambers

Absolute submission is not enough; we should go on to joyful acquiescence to the will of God.

C. H. Spurgeon

Our sense of joy, satisfaction, and fulfillment in life increases, no matter what the circumstances, if we are in the center of God's will.

Billy Graham

To walk out of His will is to walk into nowhere.

C. S. Lewis

A Christian seeking God's will must be certain that he has first relinquished control of his life, including his finances, and is truly seeking God's direction.

Larry Burkett

You cannot stay where you are and go with God. You cannot continue doing things your way and accomplish God's purposes in His ways. Your thinking cannot come close to God's thoughts. For you to do the will of God, you must adjust your life to Him, His purposes, and His ways.

Henry Blackaby

A PRAYER FOR TODAY

Heavenly Father, in these quiet moments before this busy day unfolds, I come to You. I will study Your Word and seek Your guidance. Give me the wisdom to know Your will for my life and the courage to follow wherever You may lead me, today and forever. Amen

CHAPTER 16

THE PROMISE

Love has the power to transform
your life and your relationships.

*Now these three remain: faith, hope, and love.
But the greatest of these is love.*

—

1 Corinthians 13:13 HCSB

AND THE GREATEST OF THESE . . .

Christ's words left no room for interpretation: "'Love the Lord your God with all your heart and with all your soul and with all your mind.' This is the first and greatest commandment. And the second is like it: 'Love your neighbor as yourself.' All the Law and the Prophets hang on these two commandments" (Matthew 22:37-40 NIV). But sometimes, despite our best intentions, we fall short. When we become embittered with ourselves, with our neighbors, or most especially with God, we disobey the One who gave His life for us.

If we are to please God, we must cleanse ourselves of the negative feelings that separate us from others and from Him. In 1 Corinthians 13, we are told that love is the foundation upon which all our relationships are to be built: our relationships with others and our relationship with our Maker. May we fill our hearts with love; may we never yield to bitterness. And may we praise the Son of God who, in His infinite wisdom, made love His greatest commandment.

PROMISES FROM GOD'S WORD

If I speak the languages of men and of angels, but do not have love, I am a sounding gong or a clanging cymbal.

1 Corinthians 13:1 HCSB

I pray that you, being rooted and firmly established in love, may be able to comprehend with all the saints what is the breadth and width, height and depth, and to know the Messiah's love that surpasses knowledge, so you may be filled with all the fullness of God.

Ephesians 3:17-19 HCSB

We love because He first loved us.

1 John 4:19 HCSB

Dear friends, if God loved us in this way, we also must love one another.

1 John 4:11 HCSB

A TIMELY TIP

The key to successful Christian living lies in your submission to the Spirit of God. If you're a Christian, God has commanded you to love everybody, including the saints, the sinners, and everybody in between.

Truth becomes hard if it is not softened by love, and love becomes soft if not strengthened by truth.

E. Stanley Jones

Brotherly love is still the distinguishing badge of every true Christian.

Matthew Henry

Love must be supported and fed and protected, just like a little infant who is growing up at home.

James Dobson

Beware that you are not swallowed up in books! An ounce of love is worth a pound of knowledge.

John Wesley

Forgiveness is the final form of love.

Reinhold Niebuhr

Love is not measured by what it gets, but by what it costs.

Oswald Chambers

The truth of the Gospel is intended to free us to love God and others with our whole heart.

John Eldredge

A PRAYER FOR TODAY

Dear Lord, You have given me the gift of love; let me share that gift with others. And, keep me mindful that the essence of love is not to receive it, but to give it, today and forever. Amen

CHAPTER 17

THE PROMISE

When you worship God
with an open heart and willing hands,
you will be blessed.

*But an hour is coming, and is now here, when
the true worshipers will worship the Father in
spirit and truth. Yes, the Father wants such people
to worship Him. God is Spirit, and those who
worship Him must worship in spirit and truth.*

—

John 4:23-24 HCSB

THE IMPORTANCE OF WORSHIP

All of mankind is engaged in worship of one kind or another. The question is not whether we worship, but what we worship. Some of us choose to worship God. The result is a plentiful harvest of joy, peace, and abundance. Others distance themselves from God by foolishly worshiping things of this earth such as fame, fortune, or personal gratification.

Whenever we place our love for material possessions above our love for God—or when we yield to the countless temptations of this world—we find ourselves engaged in a struggle between good and evil, a clash between God and Satan. Our responses to these struggles have implications that echo throughout our families and throughout our communities.

How can we ensure that we cast our lot with God? We do so, in part, by the practice of regular, purposeful worship in the company of fellow believers. When we worship God faithfully and fervently, we are blessed. When we fail to worship God, for whatever reason, we forfeit the spiritual gifts that He intends for us.

We must worship our Heavenly Father, not just with our words, but also with deeds. We must honor Him, praise Him, and obey Him. As we seek to find purpose and meaning for our lives, we must first seek His purpose and His will.

PROMISES FROM GOD'S WORD

So that at the name of Jesus every knee should bow—of those who are in heaven and on earth and under the earth—and every tongue should confess that Jesus Christ is Lord, to the glory of God the Father.

Philippians 2:10-11 HCSB

If anyone is thirsty, he should come to Me and drink!

John 7:37 HCSB

All the earth will worship You and sing praise to You. They will sing praise to Your name.

Psalm 66:4 HCSB

A TIMELY TIP

Worship reminds you of the awesome power of God. So worship Him daily, and allow Him to work through you every day of the week (not just on Sundays).

When God is at the center of your life, you worship. When he's not, you worry.

Rick Warren

Each time, before you intercede, be quiet first and worship God in His glory. Think of what He can do and how He delights to hear the prayers of His redeemed people. Think of your place and privilege in Christ, and expect great things!

Andrew Murray

Inside the human heart is an undeniable, spiritual instinct to commune with its Creator.

Jim Cymbala

Worship is spiritual. Our worship must be more than just outward expression, it must also take place in our spirits.

Franklin Graham

Worship is a daunting task. Each worships differently. But each should worship.

Max Lucado

Worship is not taught from the pulpit. It must be learned in the heart.

Jim Elliot

Worship is your spirit responding to God's Spirit.

Rick Warren

A PRAYER FOR TODAY

Dear Lord, today I will worship You with my thoughts, my deeds, my words, and my prayers. Amen

CHAPTER 18

THE PROMISE

Patience is rewarded by God;
impatience is not.

A patient spirit is better than a proud spirit.

—

Ecclesiastes 7:8 HCSB

THE POWER OF PATIENCE

Are you a perfectly patient fellow? If so, feel free to skip the rest of this page. But if you're not, here's something to think about: if you really want to become a more patient person, God is ready and willing to help.

The Bible promises that when you sincerely seek God's help, He will give you the things that you need—and that includes patience. But God won't force you to become a more patient person. If you want to become a more mature Christian, you've got to do some of the work yourself—and the best time to start doing that work is now.

So, if you want to gain patience and maturity, bow your head and start praying about it. Then, rest assured that with God's help, you can most certainly make yourself a more patient, understanding, mature Christian.

PROMISES FROM GOD'S WORD

Therefore the Lord is waiting to show you mercy, and is rising up to show you compassion, for the Lord is a just God. Happy are all who wait patiently for Him.

Isaiah 30:18 HCSB

Love is patient; love is kind.

1 Corinthians 13:4 HCSB

Now we exhort you, brethren, warn those who are unruly, comfort the fainthearted, uphold the weak, be patient with all.

1 Thessalonians 5:14 NKJV

My dearly loved brothers, understand this: everyone must be quick to hear, slow to speak, and slow to anger, for man's anger does not accomplish God's righteousness.

James 1:19-20 HCSB

A TIMELY TIP

Patience pays. Impatience costs. Behave accordingly.

You can't step in front of God and not get in trouble. When He says, "Go three steps," don't go four.

Charles Stanley

In the Bible, patience is not a passive acceptance of circumstances. It is a courageous perseverance in the face of suffering and difficulty.

Warren Wiersbe

In all negotiations of difficulties, a man may not look to sow and reap at once. He must prepare his business and so ripen it by degrees.

Francis Bacon

God is more patient with us than we are with ourselves.

Max Lucado

Grass that is here today and gone tomorrow does not require much time to mature. A big oak tree that lasts for generations requires much more time to grow and mature. God is concerned about your life through eternity. Allow Him to take all the time He needs to shape you for His purposes. Larger assignments will require longer periods of preparation.

Henry Blackaby

A PRAYER FOR TODAY

Dear Lord, give me wisdom and patience. When I am hurried, give me peace. When I am frustrated, give me perspective. When I am angry, keep me mindful of Your presence. Today, let me be a patient Christian, Lord, as I trust in You and in Your master plan for my life. Amen

CHAPTER 19

THE PROMISE

When you obey God,
you will be blessed today, tomorrow,
and throughout eternity.

*Therefore, get your minds ready for action, being
self-disciplined, and set your hope completely
on the grace to be brought to you at the revelation
of Jesus Christ. As obedient children, do not be
conformed to the desires of your former ignorance
but, as the One who called you is holy, you also
are to be holy in all your conduct.*

—

1 Peter 1:13-15 HCSB

OBEY HIM

We live in a world filled with temptations, distractions, and countless opportunities to disobey God. But as men who seek to be godly role models for our families, we must turn our thoughts and our hearts away from the evils of this world. We must turn instead to God.

Talking about God is easy; living by His commandments is considerably harder. But unless we are willing to abide by God's laws, our righteous proclamations ring hollow.

How can we best proclaim our love for the Lord? By obeying Him. We must seek God's counsel and trust the counsel He gives. And, when we invite God into our hearts and live according to His commandments, we are blessed today, and tomorrow, and forever.

PROMISES FROM GOD'S WORD

Therefore, everyone who hears these words of Mine and acts on them will be like a sensible man who built his house on the rock. The rain fell, the rivers rose, and the winds blew and pounded that house. Yet it didn't collapse, because its foundation was on the rock.

Matthew 7:24–25 HCSB

I have sought You with all my heart; don't let me wander from Your commands.

Psalm 119:10 HCSB

Jesus answered, "If anyone loves Me, he will keep My word. My Father will love him, and We will come to him and make Our home with him."

John 14:23 HCSB

This is how we know that we love God's children, when we love God and obey His commands.

1 John 5:2 HCSB

A TIMELY TIP

Because God is just, He rewards good behavior just as surely as He punishes sin. Obedience earns God's pleasure; disobedience doesn't.

Trials and sufferings teach us to obey the Lord by faith, and we soon learn that obedience pays off in joyful ways.

Bill Bright

When you suffer and lose, that does not mean you are being disobedient to God. In fact, it might mean you're right in the center of His will. The path of obedience is often marked by times of suffering and loss.

Charles Swindoll

Only he who believes is obedient. Only he who is obedient believes.

Dietrich Bonhoeffer

Mary could not have dreamed all that would result from her faithful obedience. Likewise, you cannot possibly imagine all that God has in store for you when you trust him.

Henry Blackaby

Obedience is the road to freedom, humility the road to pleasure, unity the road to personality.

C. S. Lewis

True faith commits us to obedience.

A. W. Tozer

A PRAYER FOR TODAY

Dear Heavenly Father, You have blessed me with a love that is infinite and eternal. Let me demonstrate my love for You by obeying Your commandments. Make me a faithful servant, Father, today and throughout eternity. And, let me show my love for You by sharing Your message and Your love with others. Amen

CHAPTER 20

THE PROMISE

When you discipline yourself,
God will bless you.

*I discipline my body and bring it under
strict control, so that after preaching to others,
I myself will not be disqualified.*

—

1 Corinthians 9:27 HCSB

THE IMPORTANCE OF DISCIPLINE

The words *disciple* and *discipline* are both derived from Latin, so it's not surprising that when you become a disciple of Christ you should expect to exercise self-discipline in all matters. Self-discipline is not simply a proven way to get ahead; it's also an integral part of God's plan for your life. So if you genuinely seek to be a faithful steward of your time, your talents, and your resources, you must adopt a disciplined approach to life. Otherwise, your talents are likely to go unused, and your resources are likely to be squandered.

Most of life's greatest rewards come as the result of hard work and perseverance. May you, as a disciplined disciple, be willing to do the work—and keep doing it—until you've earned the rewards that God has in store for you.

PROMISES FROM GOD'S WORD

For this very reason, make every effort to supplement your faith with goodness, goodness with knowledge, knowledge with self-control, self-control with endurance, endurance with godliness.

2 Peter 1:5-6 HCSB

The one who follows instruction is on the path to life, but the one who rejects correction goes astray.

Proverbs 10:17 HCSB

No discipline seems enjoyable at the time, but painful. Later on, however, it yields the fruit of peace and righteousness to those who have been trained by it.

Hebrews 12:11 HCSB

But each person should examine his own work, and then he will have a reason for boasting in himself alone, and not in respect to someone else. For each person will have to carry his own load.

Galatians 6:4-5 HCSB

A TIMELY TIP

If you choose to lead a disciplined lifestyle, your steps will be protected. If you choose to lead an undisciplined lifestyle, your steps will be misdirected.

Discipline is training that develops and corrects.

Charles Stanley

Work is doing it. Discipline is doing it every day. Diligence is doing it well every day.

Dave Ramsey

The Bible calls for discipline and a recognition of authority. Children must learn this at home.

Billy Graham

Personal humility is a spiritual discipline and the hallmark of the service of Jesus.

Franklin Graham

As we seek to become disciples of Jesus Christ, we should never forget that the word disciple is directly related to the word discipline. To be a disciple of the Lord Jesus Christ is to know his discipline.

Dennis Swanberg

The alternative to discipline is disaster.

Vance Havner

If one examines the secret behind a championship football team, a magnificent orchestra, or a successful business, the principal ingredient is invariably discipline.

James Dobson

A PRAYER FOR TODAY

Dear Lord, I want to be a disciplined believer. Let me use my time wisely, let me obey Your commandments faithfully, and let me worship You joyfully, today and every day. Amen

CHAPTER 21

THE PROMISE

If you want wisdom, God is always
ready to give it—all you must do is ask.

*Now if any of you lacks wisdom, he should ask
God, who gives to all generously and without
criticizing, and it will be given to him.*

—

James 1:5 HCSB

LIFETIME LEARNING

God does not intend for you to be a stagnant believer. Far from it! God wants you to continue growing as a person and as a Christian every day that you live. And make no mistake: both spiritual and intellectual growth are possible during every stage of life.

As a spiritual being, you have the potential to grow in your personal knowledge of the Lord every day that you live. You can do so through prayer, through worship, through an openness to God's Holy Spirit, and through a careful study of God's Holy Word. Your Bible contains powerful prescriptions for everyday living. If you sincerely seek to walk with God, you should commit yourself to the thoughtful study of His teachings.

Do you seek to live a life of righteousness and wisdom? If so, you must continue to study the ultimate source of wisdom: the Word of God. You must associate, day in and day out, with godly men and women. And, you must act in accordance with your beliefs.

When you study God's Word and live according to His commandments, you will become wise . . . and you will serve as a shining example to your friends, to your family, and to the world.

PROMISES FROM GOD'S WORD

Buy—and do not sell—truth, wisdom, instruction, and understanding.

Proverbs 23:23 HCSB

Wisdom is the principal thing; therefore get wisdom. And in all your getting, get understanding.

Proverbs 4:7 NKJV

For now we see indistinctly, as in a mirror, but then face to face. Now I know in part, but then I will know fully, as I am fully known.

1 Corinthians 13:12 HCSB

An ear that listens to life-giving rebukes will be at home among the wise.

Proverbs 15:31 HCSB

A TIMELY TIP

God still has important lessons to teach you. Your task is to be open to His instruction.

✦—✦ ✥✦✥ ✦—✦

God's plan for our guidance is for us to grow gradually in wisdom before we get to the crossroads.

Bill Hybels

Wise people listen to wise instruction, especially instruction from the Word of God.

Warren Wiersbe

Don't expect wisdom to come into your life like great chunks of rock on a conveyor belt. Wisdom comes privately from God as a by-product of right decisions, godly reactions, and the application of spiritual principles to daily circumstances.

Charles Swindoll

It's the things you learn after you know it all that really count.

Vance Havner

The wise man gives proper appreciation in his life to his past. He learns to sift the sawdust of heritage in order to find the nuggets that make the current moment have any meaning.

Grady Nutt

The vigor of our spiritual lives will be in exact proportion to the place held by the Bible in our lives and in our thoughts.

George Mueller

A PRAYER FOR TODAY

Dear Lord, I have so much to learn. Help me to watch, to listen, to think, and to learn, every day of my life. Amen

CHAPTER 22

THE PROMISE

Whenever we refuse to forgive others,
we invite God's displeasure.

*And whenever you stand praying,
if you have anything against anyone, forgive him,
so that your Father in heaven may also
forgive you your wrongdoing.*

—

Mark 11:25 HCSB

FORGIVENESS NOW

Are you the kind of man who carries a grudge? If so, you know sometimes it's very tough to forgive the people who have hurt you. And that's too bad because life would be much simpler if we could forgive people "once and for all" and be done with it. But forgiveness is seldom that easy. Forgiveness is a journey that requires effort, time, perseverance, and prayer.

Forgiveness is seldom easy, but it is always right. When we forgive those who have hurt us, we honor God by obeying His commandments. But when we harbor bitterness against others, we disobey God—with predictably unhappy results.

If there exists even one person whom you have not forgiven (and that includes yourself), follow God's commandment and His will for your life: forgive that person today. And remember that bitterness, anger, and regret are not part of God's plan for your life. Forgiveness is.

If you sincerely wish to forgive someone, pray for that person. And then pray for yourself by asking God to heal your heart. Don't expect forgiveness to be easy or quick, but rest assured:

with God as your partner, you can forgive . . . and you will.

PROMISES FROM GOD'S WORD

A person's insight gives him patience, and his virtue is to overlook an offense.

Proverbs 19:11 HCSB

See to it that no one repays evil for evil to anyone, but always pursue what is good for one another and for all.

1 Thessalonians 5:15 HCSB

And forgive us our sins, for we ourselves also forgive everyone in debt to us.

Luke 11:4 HCSB

Be merciful, just as your Father also is merciful.

Luke 6:36 HCSB

A TIMELY TIP

Forgiveness is its own reward. Bitterness is its own punishment. Guard your words and your thoughts accordingly.

By not forgiving, by not letting wrongs go, we aren't getting back at anyone. We are merely punishing ourselves by barricading our own hearts.

Jim Cymbala

To hold on to hate and resentments is to throw a monkey wrench into the machinery of life.

E. Stanley Jones

Our forgiveness toward others should flow from a realization and appreciation of God's forgiveness toward us.

Franklin Graham

Give me such love for God and men as will blot out all hatred and bitterness.

Dietrich Bonhoeffer

The love of God is revealed in that He laid down His life for His enemies.

Oswald Chambers

Miracles broke the physical laws of the universe; forgiveness broke the moral rules.

Philip Yancey

A PRAYER FOR TODAY

Heavenly Father, give me a forgiving heart. When I am bitter, Your Word reminds me that forgiveness is Your commandment. Let me be Your obedient servant, Lord, and let me be a man who forgives others just as You have forgiven me. Amen

CHAPTER 23

THE PROMISE

When you are a faithful steward
of the gifts God has given you,
He will entrust you with more.

*Well done, good and faithful servant;
you were faithful over a few things,
I will make you ruler over many things.
Enter into the joy of your lord.*

—

Matthew 25:21 NKJV

BEING A FAITHFUL STEWARD

Do you seek to be a righteous follower of Christ? Do you earnestly seek God's will for your life? And do you trust God's promises? If so, then you will be a faithful steward of the gifts He has given you.

Oswald Chambers advised, "Never support an experience which does not have God as its source, and faith in God as its result." And so it is with our tithes. When we return to God that which is rightfully His, we experience the spiritual growth that always accompanies obedience to Him. But, when we attempt to shortchange our Creator, either materially or spiritually, we distance ourselves from God. The consequences of our disobedience are as predictable as they are tragic.

As Christians, we are called to walk with God and to obey His commandments. To do so is an act of holiness. God deserves our obedience. May we obey Him in all things, including our tithes.

PROMISES FROM GOD'S WORD

Let a man so consider us, as servants of Christ and stewards of the mysteries of God. Moreover it is required in stewards that one be found faithful.

1 Corinthians 4:1-2 NKJV

Based on the gift they have received, everyone should use it to serve others, as good managers of the varied grace of God.

1 Peter 4:10 HCSB

He that giveth, let him do it with simplicity.

Romans 12:8 KJV

For I am the Lord, I do not change. Will a man rob God? Yet you have robbed Me! But you say, in what way have we robbed You? In tithes and offerings. You are cursed with a curse, for you have robbed Me, even this whole nation. Bring all the tithes into the storehouse, that there may be food in My house.

Malachi 3:6, 8-10 NKJV

A TIMELY TIP

God's Word makes it clear: during good times and hard times, you are instructed to be a faithful steward of your talents, your time, and your resources.

We are never more like God than when we give.

Charles Swindoll

Christians have become victims of one of the most devious plots Satan ever created—the concept that money belongs to us and not to God.

Larry Burkett

If our charities do not at all pinch or hamper us, I should say they are too small. There ought to be things we should like to do and cannot do because our charitable expenditure excludes them.

C. S. Lewis

A steward does not own, but instead manages, all that his master puts into his hands.

Warren Wiersbe

Selfishness is as far from Christianity as darkness is from light.

C. H. Spurgeon

You can sing your heart out but never give back to God, and you'll miss the fullness of worship.

Dave Ramsey

A PRAYER FOR TODAY

Dear Lord, make me a faithful steward of my possessions, my talents, my time, and my testimony. In every aspect of my life, Father, let me be Your humble, obedient servant. I trust, Father, that You will provide for me now and throughout eternity. And I will obey Your commandment that I give sacrificially to the needs of Your Church. Amen

CHAPTER 24

THE PROMISE

God intends for you to experience
His joy now and forever.

*Now I am coming to You, and I speak these things
in the world so that they may have
My joy completed in them.*

—

John 17:13 HCSB

REJOICE ALWAYS

Have you made the choice to rejoice? Hopefully so. After all, if you're a believer, you have plenty of reasons to be joyful. Yet sometimes, amid the inevitable hustle and bustle of life here on earth, you may lose sight of your blessings as you wrestle with the challenges of everyday life.

Psalm 100 reminds us that, as believers, we have every reason to celebrate: "Shout for joy to the LORD, all the earth. Worship the LORD with gladness" (vv. 1-2 NIV). Yet sometimes, we can forfeit—albeit temporarily—the joy that God intends for our lives.

If you find yourself feeling discouraged or worse, it's time to slow down and have a quiet conversation with your Creator. If your heart is heavy, open the door of your soul to the Father and to His only begotten Son. Christ offers you His peace and His joy. Accept it and share it freely, just as Christ has freely shared His joy with you.

PROMISES FROM GOD'S WORD

Rejoice in the Lord always. I will say it again: Rejoice!

Philippians 4:4 HCSB

Make me to hear joy and gladness.

Psalm 51:8 KJV

So you also have sorrow now. But I will see you again. Your hearts will rejoice, and no one will rob you of your joy.

John 16:22 HCSB

Weeping may spend the night, but there is joy in the morning.

Psalm 30:5 HCSB

Glory in His holy name; Let the hearts of those rejoice who seek the Lord! Seek the Lord and His strength; Seek His face evermore!

1 Chronicles 16:10-11 NKJV

A TIMELY TIP

Joy begins with a choice—the choice to establish a genuine relationship with God and His Son. Joy does not depend upon your circumstances, but upon your relationship with God.

Gratitude changes the pangs of memory into a tranquil joy.

Dietrich Bonhoeffer

Joy is the direct result of having God's perspective on our daily lives and the effect of loving our Lord enough to obey His commands and trust His promises.

Bill Bright

We all sin by needlessly disobeying the apostolic injunction to rejoice.

C. S. Lewis

The ability to rejoice in any situation is a sign of spiritual maturity.

Billy Graham

Today you will encounter God's creation. When you see the beauty around you, let each detail remind you to lift your head in praise.

Max Lucado

Rejoice, the Lord is King; Your Lord and King adore! Rejoice, give thanks and sing and triumph evermore.

Charles Wesley

A PRAYER FOR TODAY

Dear Lord, You are my loving Heavenly Father, and You created me in Your image. As Your faithful child, I will make Your joy my joy. I will praise Your works, I will obey Your Word, and I will honor Your Son, this day and every day of my life. Amen

CHAPTER 25

THE PROMISE

God's love for you will never end.

*Praise the Lord, all nations! Glorify Him,
all peoples! For great is His faithful love to us;
the Lord's faithfulness endures forever. Hallelujah!*

—

Psalm 117 HCSB

PRAISE HIM EVERY DAY

When is the best time to praise God? In church? Before dinner is served? When we tuck little children into bed? None of the above. The best time to praise God is all day, every day, to the greatest extent we can, with thanksgiving in our hearts.

Too many of us, even well-intentioned believers, tend to "compartmentalize" our waking hours into a few familiar categories: work, rest, play, family time, and worship. To do so is a mistake. Worship and praise should be woven into the fabric of everything we do; it should never be relegated to a weekly three-hour visit to church on Sunday morning.

Mrs. Charles E. Cowman, the author of the classic devotional text, *Streams in the Desert,* wrote, "Two wings are necessary to lift our souls toward God: prayer and praise. Prayer asks. Praise accepts the answer." Today, find a little more time to lift your concerns to God in prayer, and praise Him for all that He has done. He's listening . . . and He wants to hear from you.

PROMISES FROM GOD'S WORD

Therefore, through Him let us continually offer up to God a sacrifice of praise, that is, the fruit of our lips that confess His name.

Hebrews 13:15 HCSB

But I will hope continually and will praise You more and more.

Psalm 71:14 HCSB

Enter into his gates with thanksgiving, and into his courts with praise: be thankful unto him, and bless his name. For the LORD is good; his mercy is everlasting; and his truth endureth to all generations.

Psalm 100:4-5 KJV

And suddenly there was with the angel a multitude of the heavenly host praising God and saying: "Glory to God in the highest, And on earth peace, goodwill toward men!"

Luke 2:13-14 NKJV

A TIMELY TIP

Remember that it always pays to praise your Creator. That's why thoughtful believers (like you) make it a habit to carve out quiet moments throughout the day to praise God.

It is only with gratitude that life becomes rich.

Dietrich Bonhoeffer

Why wait until the fourth Thursday in November? Why wait until the morning of December twenty-fifth? Thanksgiving to God should be an everyday affair. The time to be thankful is now!

Jim Gallery

The words "thank" and "think" come from the same root word. If we would think more, we would thank more.

Warren Wiersbe

A child of God should be a visible beatitude for joy and a living doxology for gratitude.

C. H. Spurgeon

Thank God every morning when you get up that you have something to do that day which must be done, whether you like it or not.

Charles Kingsley

Holy, holy, holy! Lord God Almighty! All Thy works shall praise Thy name in earth, and sky, and sea.

Reginald Heber

A PRAYER FOR TODAY

Dear Lord, make me a man who gives constant praise to You. And, let me share the joyous news of Jesus Christ with a world that needs His transformation and His salvation. Amen

CHAPTER 26

THE PROMISE

God's truth can liberate your spirit
and transform your life.

*You will know the truth,
and the truth will set you free.*

—

John 8:32 HCSB

SEARCHING FOR TRUTH

Would you like a rock-solid, time-tested formula for success? Here it is: seek God's truth, and live by it. Of course this strategy may sound simple, and it may sound somewhat old-fashioned, especially if you're a fast-track, dues-paying citizen of the 21st century. But God's truth never goes out of style. And God's wisdom is as valid today as it was when He laid the foundations of the universe.

The familiar words of John 8:32 remind us that "you shall know the truth, and the truth shall make you free" (NKJV). And St. Augustine had this advice: "Let everything perish! Dismiss these empty vanities! And let us take up the search for the truth."

God is vitally concerned with truth. His Word teaches the truth; His Spirit reveals the truth; His Son leads us to the truth. When we open our hearts to God, and when we allow His Son to rule over our thoughts and our lives, God reveals Himself, and we come to understand the truth about ourselves and the truth about God's gift of grace.

Are you seeking God's truth and making decisions in light of that truth? Hopefully so. When you do, you'll discover that the truth will indeed set you free, now and forever.

PROMISES FROM GOD'S WORD

Be diligent to present yourself approved to God, a worker who doesn't need to be ashamed, correctly teaching the word of truth.

2 Timothy 2:15 HCSB

You have already heard about this hope in the message of truth, the gospel that has come to you. It is bearing fruit and growing all over the world, just as it has among you since the day you heard it and recognized God's grace in the truth.

Colossians 1:5-6 HCSB

When the Spirit of truth comes, He will guide you into all the truth.

John 16:13 HCSB

A TIMELY TIP

Warren Wiersbe writes, "Learning God's truth and getting it into our heads is one thing, but living God's truth and getting it into our characters is quite something else." So don't be satisfied to sit on the sidelines and observe the truth at a distance—live it.

Lying covers a multitude of sins—temporarily.

D. L. Moody

You cannot glorify Christ and practice deception at the same time.

Warren Wiersbe

The only people who achieve much are those who want knowledge so badly that they seek it while the conditions are still unfavorable. Favorable conditions never come.

C. S. Lewis

Honesty has a beautiful and refreshing simplicity about it. No ulterior motives. No hidden meanings. As honesty and integrity characterize our lives, there will be no need to manipulate others.

Charles Swindoll

For Christians, God himself is the only absolute; truth and ethics are rooted in his character.

Chuck Colson

We have in Jesus Christ a perfect example of how to put God's truth into practice.

Bill Bright

A PRAYER FOR TODAY

Dear Lord, Jesus said He was the Truth, and I believe Him. Father, may Jesus always be the standard for truth in my life so that I might be a worthy example to others and a worthy servant to You. Amen

CHAPTER 27

THE PROMISE

God's blessings, like His love,
never end.

*My cup runs over. Surely goodness and mercy
shall follow me all the days of my life;
and I will dwell in the house of the Lord forever.*

—

Psalm 23:5-6 NKJV

COUNTING YOUR BLESSINGS

If you sat down and began counting your blessings, how long would it take? A very, very long time! Your blessings include life, freedom, family, friends, talents, and possessions, for starters. But, your greatest blessing—a gift that is yours for the asking—is God's gift of salvation through Christ Jesus.

We honor God, in part, by the genuine gratitude we feel in our hearts for the blessings He has bestowed upon us. Yet even the most saintly among us must endure periods of fear, doubt, and regret. Why? Because we are imperfect human beings who are incapable of perfect gratitude. Still, even on life's darker days, we must seek to cleanse our hearts of negative emotions and fill them, instead, with praise, with love, with hope, and with thanksgiving. To do otherwise is to be unfair to ourselves, to our loved ones, and to our God.

Today, begin making a list of your blessings. You most certainly will not be able to make a complete list, but take a few moments and jot down as many blessings as you can. Then, give thanks to the Giver of all good things: God. His love for you is eternal, as are His gifts. And it's never too soon—or too late—to offer Him thanks.

PROMISES FROM GOD'S WORD

You will show me the path of life; in Your presence is fullness of joy; at Your right hand are pleasures forevermore.

Psalm 16:11 NKJV

Blessed is a man who endures trials, because when he passes the test he will receive the crown of life that He has promised to those who love Him.

James 1:12 HCSB

I will make you a great nation; I will bless you and make your name great; and you shall be a blessing. I will bless those who bless you, and I will curse him who curses you; and in you all the families of the earth shall be blessed.

Genesis 12:2-3 NKJV

A TIMELY TIP

God wants to bless you abundantly and eternally. When you trust God completely and obey Him faithfully, you will be blessed.

With the goodness of God to desire our highest welfare and the wisdom of God to plan it, what do we lack? Surely we are the most favored of all creatures.

A. W. Tozer

Grace is an outrageous blessing bestowed freely on a totally undeserving recipient.

Bill Hybels

The Christian life is motivated, not by a list of dos and don'ts, but by the gracious outpouring of God's love and blessing.

Anne Graham Lotz

It is when we give ourselves to be a blessing that we can specially count on the blessing of God.

Andrew Murray

Blessings can either humble us and draw us closer to God or allow us to become full of pride and self-sufficiency.

Jim Cymbala

God blesses us in spite of our lives and not because of our lives.

Max Lucado

A PRAYER FOR TODAY

Lord, You have given me so much, and I am thankful. Today, I seek Your blessings for my life, and I know that every good thing You give me is to be shared with others. I am blessed that I might be a blessing to those around me, Father. Let me give thanks for Your gifts . . . and let me share them. Amen

CHAPTER 28

THE PROMISE

When you worship God and follow in the footsteps of His Son, you have every reason to be hopeful about your life and your eternal future.

For I know the thoughts that I think toward you, says the Lord, thoughts of peace and not of evil, to give you a future and a hope. Then you will call upon Me and go and pray to Me, and I will listen to you.

—

Jeremiah 29:11-12 NKJV

BE HOPEFUL

Look around you. Read the newspaper. Watch the evening news. When you think about the things that are going on in Washington or elsewhere in the world, it's possible to lose hope. But God provides an antidote to despair. One of the rewards of spending time before the face of God is the gift of divine hope.

Have you ever felt your hope in the future slipping away? If so, here's what you should do: study God's Word, seek God's will, and spend prayerful hours before God's face. When you do, you'll discover the hope that is the possession of those who place their trust in Him.

This world can be a place of trials and tribulations, but as believers in Christ we are secure. We need never lose hope, because God has promised us peace, joy, and eternal life. So, let us face each day with hope in our hearts and trust in our God. And, let us teach our children to do likewise. After all, God has promised us that we are His throughout eternity, and He keeps His promises. Always.

PROMISES FROM GOD'S WORD

Now may the God of hope fill you with all joy and peace in believing, so that you may overflow with hope by the power of the Holy Spirit.

Romans 15:13 HCSB

But if we hope for what we do not see, we eagerly wait for it with patience.

Romans 8:25 HCSB

Rejoice in hope; be patient in affliction; be persistent in prayer.

Romans 12:12 HCSB

Lord, I turn my hope to You. My God, I trust in You. Do not let me be disgraced; do not let my enemies gloat over me.

Psalm 25:1-2 HCSB

Let us hold on to the confession of our hope without wavering, for He who promised is faithful.

Hebrews 10:23 HCSB

A TIMELY TIP

Never be afraid to hope—or to ask—for a miracle.

People are genuinely motivated by hope, and a part of that hope is the assurance of future glory with God for those who are His people.

Warren Wiersbe

Our hope in Christ for the future is the mainstream of our joy.

C. H. Spurgeon

Oh, remember this: There is never a time when we may not hope in God. Whatever our necessities, however great our difficulties, and though to all appearance help is impossible, yet our business is to hope in God, and it will be found that it is not in vain.

George Mueller

The hope we have in Jesus is the anchor for the soul—something sure and steadfast, preventing drifting or giving way, lowered to the depth of God's love.

Franklin Graham

Faith looks back and draws courage; hope looks ahead and keeps desire alive.

John Eldredge

Hope is nothing more than the expectation of those things which faith has believed to be truly promised by God.

John Calvin

A PRAYER FOR TODAY

Dear Lord, make me a man of hope. If I become discouraged, let me turn to You. When I face adversity, let me seek Your will and trust Your Word. In every aspect of my life, I will trust You, Father, so that my heart will be filled with faith and hope, this day and forever. Amen

CHAPTER 29

THE PROMISE

God offers peace that surpasses
human understanding.

*The peace of God, which surpasses
all understanding, will guard your hearts
and minds through Christ Jesus.*

—

Philippians 4:7 NKJV

FINDING PEACE

Our world is in a state of constant change and so are we. God is not. At times, everything around us seems to be changing: our children are growing up, we are growing older, loved ones pass on. Sometimes, the world seems to be trembling beneath our feet. But we can be comforted in the knowledge that our Heavenly Father is the Rock that cannot be shaken.

Are you at peace with the direction of your life? If you're a Christian, you should be. Perhaps you seek a new direction or a sense of renewed purpose, but those feelings should never rob you of the genuine peace that can and should be yours through a personal relationship with Jesus. The demands of everyday living should never obscure the fact that Christ died so that you might have life abundant and eternal.

Have you found the lasting peace that can be yours through Jesus, or are you still rushing after the illusion of "peace and happiness" that our world promises but cannot deliver? The world's "peace" is fleeting; Christ's peace is forever.

Christ is standing at the door, waiting patiently for you to invite Him to reign in your heart. His eternal peace is offered freely. Claim it today.

PROMISES FROM GOD'S WORD

Abundant peace belongs to those who love Your instruction; nothing makes them stumble.

Psalm 119:165 HCSB

If possible, on your part, live at peace with everyone.

Romans 12:18 HCSB

Blessed are the peacemakers, for they shall be called sons of God.

Matthew 5:9 NKJV

So then, we must pursue what promotes peace and what builds up one another.

Romans 14:19 HCSB

A TIMELY TIP

God's peace surpasses human understanding. When you accept His peace, it will revolutionize your life.

That peace, which has been described and which believers enjoy, is a participation of the peace which their glorious Lord and Master himself enjoys.

Jonathan Edwards

Peace is the deepest thing a human personality can know; it is almighty.

Oswald Chambers

We're prone to want God to change our circumstances, but He wants to change our character. We think that peace comes from the outside in, but it comes from the inside out.

Warren Wiersbe

What peace can they have who are not at peace with God?

Matthew Henry

A great many people are trying to make peace, but that has already been done. God has not left it for us to do; all we have to do is to enter into it.

D. L. Moody

He keeps us in perfect peace while He whispers His secrets and reveals His counsels.

Oswald Chambers

Peace with God is where all peace begins.

Jim Gallery

A PRAYER FOR TODAY

Dear Lord, You give me peace. I thank You, Father, for Your love, for Your peace, and for Your Son. Amen

CHAPTER 30

THE PROMISE

God rewards those who serve Him
with enthusiasm.

Whatever you do, do it enthusiastically,
as something done for the Lord and not for men.

—

Colossians 3:23 HCSB

ENTHUSIASM FOR THE JOURNEY

Can you truthfully say that you are an enthusiastic person? Are you passionate about your faith, your life, your family, and your future? Hopefully so. But if your zest for life has waned, it is now time to redirect your efforts and recharge your spiritual batteries. And that means refocusing your priorities by putting God first.

Each day is a glorious opportunity to serve God and to do His will. Are you enthused about life, or do you struggle through each day giving scarcely a thought to God's blessings? Are you constantly praising God for His gifts, and are you sharing His Good News with the world? And are you excited about the possibilities for service that God has placed before you, whether at home, at work, or at church? You should be.

Nothing is more important than your wholehearted commitment to your Creator and to His only begotten Son. Your faith must never be an afterthought; it must be your ultimate priority, your ultimate possession, and your ultimate passion. When you become passionate about your faith, you'll become passionate about your life, too.

PROMISES FROM GOD'S WORD

I have seen that there is nothing better than for a person to enjoy his activities, because that is his reward. For who can enable him to see what will happen after he dies?

Ecclesiastes 3:22 HCSB

Do not lack diligence; be fervent in spirit; serve the Lord.

Romans 12:11 HCSB

He did it with all his heart. So he prospered.

2 Chronicles 31:21 NKJV

Render service with a good attitude, as to the Lord and not to men.

Ephesians 6:7 HCSB

A TIMELY TIP

Don't wait for enthusiasm to find you . . .
go looking for it. Look at your life and your
relationships as exciting adventures. Don't wait
for life to spice up itself; spice things up yourself.

Don't take hold of a thing unless you want that
thing to take hold of you.

E. Stanley Jones

When we wholeheartedly commit ourselves to
God, there is nothing mediocre or run-of-the-
mill about us. To live for Christ is to be passionate
about our Lord and about our lives.

Jim Gallery

One of the great needs in the church today is for
every Christian to become enthusiastic about his
faith in Jesus Christ.

Billy Graham

Enthusiasm, like the flu, is contagious—we get it from one another.

Barbara Johnson

Wherever you are, be all there. Live to the hilt every situation you believe to be the will of God.

Jim Elliot

Catch on fire with enthusiasm and people will come for miles to watch you burn.

John Wesley

A PRAYER FOR TODAY

Dear Lord, make me a source of genuine, lasting encouragement to my family and friends. Today, I will celebrate Your blessings, and I will share Your Good News with those who cross my path. Let my words and deeds be worthy of Your Son, the One who gives me strength and salvation. Amen

CHAPTER 31

THE PROMISE

God love for you is infinite
and everlasting.

The one who trusts in the Lord
will have faithful love surrounding him.

—

Psalm 32:10 HCSB

EMBRACED BY GOD

God's love for you is bigger and better than you can imagine. In fact, God's love is far too big to comprehend. But this much we know: God loves you so much that He sent His Son Jesus to come to this earth and to die for you. And, when you accepted Jesus into your heart, God gave you a gift that is more precious than gold: the gift of eternal life.

The words of Romans 8 make this promise: "For I am persuaded that neither death nor life, nor angels nor principalities nor powers, nor things present nor things to come, nor height nor depth, nor any other created thing, shall be able to separate us from the love of God which is in Christ Jesus our Lord" (vv. 38-39 NKJV).

Sometimes, in the crush of your daily duties, God may seem far away, but He is not. God is everywhere you have ever been and everywhere you will ever go. He is with you night and day; He knows your thoughts and He hears your prayers. When you earnestly seek Him, you will find Him because He is here, waiting patiently for you to reach out to Him.

Reach out to God today and always. Encourage your family members to do likewise. And then, arm-in-arm with your loved ones, praise God for blessings that are simply too numerous to count.

PROMISES FROM GOD'S WORD

For the Lord is good, and His love is eternal; His faithfulness endures through all generations.

Psalm 100:5 HCSB

Help me, Lord my God; save me according to Your faithful love.

Psalm 109:26 HCSB

Whoever is wise will observe these things, and they will understand the lovingkindness of the Lord.

Psalm 107:43 NKJV

A person's insight gives him patience, and his virtue is to overlook an offense.

Proverbs 19:11 HCSB

A TIMELY TIP

Remember: God's love for you is too big to understand with your brain . . . but it's not too big to feel with your heart.

Though we may not act like our Father, there is no greater truth than this: We are his. Unalterably. He loves us. Undyingly. Nothing can separate us from the love of Christ.

Max Lucado

Even when we cannot see the why and wherefore of God's dealings, we know that there is love in and behind them, so we can rejoice always.

J. I. Packer

Love so amazing, so divine, demands my soul, my life, my all.

Isaac Watts

Incomprehensible and immutable is the love of God. For it was not after we were reconciled to him by the blood of his Son that he began to love us, but he loved us before the foundation of the world, that with his only begotten Son we too might be sons of God before we were any thing at all.

St. Augustine

God has pursued us from farther than space and longer than time.

John Eldredge

There is no pit so deep that God's love is not deeper still.

Corrie ten Boom

A PRAYER FOR TODAY

Lord, I know that You love me. I will accept Your love—and share it—today and every day. Amen

CHAPTER 32

THE PROMISE

When you trust God completely,
you have every reason to be optimistic
about your life and your future.

Be strong and courageous,
all you who put your hope in the LORD.

—

Psalm 31:24 HCSB

OPTIMISM NOW

Pessimism and Christianity don't mix. Why? Because Christians have every reason to be optimistic about life here on earth and life eternal. Mrs. Charles E. Cowman advised, "Never yield to gloomy anticipation. Place your hope and confidence in God. He has no record of failure."

Sometimes, despite our trust in God, we may fall into the spiritual traps of worry, frustration, anxiety, or sheer exhaustion, and our hearts become heavy. What's needed is plenty of rest, a large dose of perspective, and God's healing touch, but not necessarily in that order.

Today, make this promise to yourself and keep it: vow to be a hope-filled Christian. Think optimistically about your life, your profession, and your future. Trust your hopes, not your fears. Take time to celebrate God's glorious creation. And then, when you've filled your heart with hope and gladness, share your optimism with others. They'll be better for it, and so will you. But not necessarily in that order.

PROMISES FROM GOD'S WORD

My cup runs over. Surely goodness and mercy shall follow me all the days of my life; and I will dwell in the house of the Lord Forever.

Psalm 23:5-6 NKJV

But if we hope for what we do not see, we eagerly wait for it with patience.

Romans 8:25 HCSB

For God has not given us a spirit of fearfulness, but one of power, love, and sound judgment.

2 Timothy 1:7 HCSB

Finally brothers, whatever is true, whatever is honorable, whatever is just, whatever is pure, whatever is lovely, whatever is commendable— if there is any moral excellence and if there is any praise—dwell on these things.

Philippians 4:8 HCSB

A TIMELY TIP

Be positive: if your thoughts tend toward the negative end of the spectrum, redirect them. How? You can start by counting your blessings and by thanking your Father in heaven. And while you're at it, train yourself to begin thinking thoughts that are more rational, more accepting, and more upbeat.

The Christian lifestyle is not one of legalistic dos and don'ts, but one that is positive, attractive, and joyful.

Vonette Bright

It never hurts your eyesight to look on the bright side of things.

Barbara Johnson

Change your thoughts, and you change your world.

Norman Vincent Peale

We may run, walk, stumble, drive, or fly, but let us never lose sight of the reason for the journey, or miss a chance to see a rainbow on the way.

Gloria Gaither

Christ can put a spring in your step and a thrill in your heart. Optimism and cheerfulness are products of knowing Christ.

Billy Graham

Make the least of all that goes and the most of all that comes. Don't regret what is past. Cherish what you have. Look forward to all that is to come. And most important of all, rely moment by moment on Jesus Christ.

Gigi Graham Tchividjian

A PRAYER FOR TODAY

Dear Lord, I will look for the best in other people, I will expect the best from You, and I will try my best to do my best—today and every day. Amen

CHAPTER 33

THE PROMISE

God is always with you,
and He always hears your prayers.

Draw near to God, and He will draw near to you.

—

James 4:8 HCSB

SENSING GOD'S PRESENCE

Since God is everywhere, we are free to sense His presence whenever we take the time to quiet our souls and turn our prayers to Him. But sometimes, amid the incessant demands of everyday life, we turn our thoughts far from God; when we do, we suffer.

Do you set aside quiet moments each day to offer praise to your Creator? As a man who has received the gift of God's grace, you most certainly should. Silence is a gift that you give to yourself and to God. During these moments of stillness, you will often sense the infinite love and power of your Creator—and He, in turn, will speak directly to your heart.

The familiar words of Psalm 46:10 remind us to "be still, and know that I am God." When we do so, we encounter the awesome presence of our loving Heavenly Father, and we are comforted in the knowledge that God is not just near. He is here.

PROMISES FROM GOD'S WORD

You will seek Me and find Me when you search for Me with all your heart.

Jeremiah 29:13 HCSB

The Lord is near all who call out to Him, all who call out to Him with integrity. He fulfills the desires of those who fear Him; He hears their cry for help and saves them.

Psalm 145:18-19 HCSB

Surely goodness and mercy shall follow me all the days of my life: and I will dwell in the house of the Lord for ever.

Psalm 23:6 KJV

I am not alone, because the Father is with Me.

John 16:32 HCSB

I have set the Lord always before me; because He is at my right hand I shall not be moved.

Psalm 16:8 NKJV

A TIMELY TIP

If you're here, God is here. If you're there, God is, too. You can't get away from Him or His love . . . thank goodness!

We need never shout across the spaces to an absent God. He is nearer than our own soul, closer than our most secret thoughts.

A. W. Tozer

The Lord Jesus by His Holy Spirit is with me, and the knowledge of His presence dispels the darkness and allays any fears.

Bill Bright

The world, space, and all visible components reverberate with God's Presence and demonstrate His Mighty Power.

Franklin Graham

It is God to whom and with whom we travel, and while He is the End of our journey, He is also at every stopping place.

Elisabeth Elliot

Let this be your chief object in prayer: to realize the presence of your heavenly Father. Let your watchword be: Alone with God.

Andrew Murray

Our souls were made to live in an upper atmosphere, and we stifle and choke if we live on any lower level. Our eyes were made to look off from these heavenly heights, and our vision is distorted by any lower gazing.

Hannah Whitall Smith

A PRAYER FOR TODAY

Dear Lord, You are always with me. Thank You for never leaving my side, even for a moment! Amen

CHAPTER 34

THE PROMISE

God will renew your strength
and your spirit if you let Him.

*I will give you a new heart
and put a new spirit within you.*

—

Ezekiel 36:26 HCSB

HE RENEWS

For busy men living in our fast-paced modern world, life may seem like a merry-go-round that never stops turning. If that description seems to fit your life, then you may find yourself running short of patience, or strength, or both. If you're feeling tired or discouraged, there is a source from which you can draw the power needed to recharge your spiritual batteries. That source is God.

Are you exhausted or troubled? Turn your heart toward God in prayer. Are you weak or worried? Take the time—or, more accurately, make the time—to delve deeply into God's Holy Word. Are you spiritually depleted? Call upon fellow believers to support you, and call upon Christ to renew your spirit and your life. When you do, you'll discover that the Creator of the universe stands always ready and always able to create a new sense of wonderment and joy in you.

PROMISES FROM GOD'S WORD

But may the God of all grace, who called us to His eternal glory by Christ Jesus, after you have suffered a while, perfect, establish, strengthen, and settle you.

1 Peter 5:10 NKJV

Finally, brothers, rejoice. Be restored, be encouraged, be of the same mind, be at peace, and the God of love and peace will be with you.

2 Corinthians 13:11 HCSB

Do not remember the former things, nor consider the things of old. Behold, I will do a new thing.

Isaiah 43:18-19 NKJV

Therefore if anyone is in Christ, he is a new creature; the old things passed away; behold, new things have come.

2 Corinthians 5:17 HCSB

A TIMELY TIP

God is in the business of making all things new: Vance Havner correctly observed, "God is not running an antique shop! He is making all things new!" And that includes you.

Walking with God leads to receiving his intimate counsel, and counseling leads to deep restoration.

John Eldredge

Troubles we bear trustfully can bring us a fresh vision of God and a new outlook on life, an outlook of peace and hope.

Billy Graham

For centuries now, Christians have poured out their hearts to the Lord and found treasured moments of refuge.

Bill Hybels

The same voice that brought Lazarus out of the tomb raised us to newness of life.

C. H. Spurgeon

When we invite Jesus into our lives, we experience life in the fullest, most vital sense.

Catherine Marshall

Our Father will refresh us with many pleasant inns on the journey, but he would not encourage us to mistake them for home.

C. S. Lewis

A PRAYER FOR TODAY

Lord, I am an imperfect man. Because my faith is limited, I may become overwhelmed by the demands of the day. When I feel tired or discouraged, renew my strength. When I am worried, let me turn my thoughts and my prayers to You. Let me trust Your promises, Dear Lord, and let me accept Your unending love, now and forever. Amen

CHAPTER 35

THE PROMISE

This day, like every other day
of your life, is a gift from God.

This is the day the LORD has made;
we will rejoice and be glad in it.

—

Psalm 118:24 NKJV

THIS IS THE DAY

The familiar words of Psalm 118:24 remind us of a profound yet simple truth: God created this day, and it's up to each of us to rejoice and to be grateful.

For Christian believers, every day begins and ends with God and His Son. Christ came to this earth to give us abundant life and eternal salvation. We give thanks to our Maker when we treasure each day and use it to the fullest.

This day is a gift from God. How will you use it? Will you celebrate God's gifts and obey His commandments? Will you share words of encouragement and hope with all who cross your path? Will you share the Good News of the risen Christ? Will you trust in the Father and praise His glorious handiwork? The answer to these questions will determine, to a surprising extent, the direction and the quality of your day.

So whatever this day holds for you, begin it and end it with God as your partner and Christ as your Savior. And throughout the day, give thanks to the One who created you and saved you. God's love for you is infinite. Accept it joyously.

PROMISES FROM GOD'S WORD

Working together with Him, we also appeal to you: "Don't receive God's grace in vain." For He says: In an acceptable time, I heard you, and in the day of salvation, I helped you. Look, now is the acceptable time; look, now is the day of salvation.

2 Corinthians 6:1-2 HCSB

I must work the works of Him who sent Me while it is day; the night is coming when no one can work.

John 9:4 NKJV

Therefore, get your minds ready for action, being self-disciplined, and set your hope completely on the grace to be brought to you at the revelation of Jesus Christ.

1 Peter 1:13 HCSB

But encourage each other daily, while it is still called today, so that none of you is hardened by sin's deception.

Hebrews 3:13 HCSB

A TIMELY TIP

If you don't feel like celebrating, start counting your blessings. Before long, you'll realize that you have plenty of reasons to celebrate.

As Christians, we must live a day at a time. No person, no matter how wealthy or gifted, can live two days at a time. God provides for us day by day.

Warren Wiersbe

He that fears not the future may enjoy the present.

Thomas Fuller

If you can forgive the person you were, accept the person you are, and believe in the person you will become, you are headed for joy. So celebrate your life.

Barbara Johnson

With each new dawn, life delivers a package to your front door, rings your doorbell, and runs.

Charles Swindoll

If we are ever going to be or do anything for our Lord, now is the time.

Vance Havner

Submit each day to God, knowing that He is God over all your tomorrows.

Kay Arthur

A PRAYER FOR TODAY

Dear Lord, You have given me another day of life; let me celebrate this day, and let me use it according to Your plan. I come to You today with faith in my heart and praise on my lips. I praise You, Father, for the gift of life and for the friends and family members who make my life rich. Enable me to live each moment to the fullest, totally involved in Your will. Amen

CHAPTER 36

THE PROMISE

To please God and to secure
His richest blessings,
you need a strong faith.

*Now without faith it is impossible to please God,
for the one who draws near to Him must believe
that He exists and rewards those who seek Him.*

—

Hebrews 11:6 HCSB

FAITH IN THE FATHER

A suffering woman sought healing in an unusual way: she simply touched the hem of Jesus' garment. When she did, Jesus turned and said, "Daughter, be of good comfort; thy faith hath made thee whole" (Matthew 9:22 KJV). We, too, can be made whole when we place our faith completely and unwaveringly in the person of Jesus Christ.

Concentration camp survivor Corrie ten Boom relied on faith during ten months of imprisonment and torture. Later, despite the fact that four of her family members had died in Nazi death camps, Corrie's faith was unshaken. She wrote, "There is no pit so deep that God's love is not deeper still." Christians take note: genuine faith in God means faith in all circumstances, happy or sad, joyful or tragic.

When you place your faith, your trust, indeed your life in the hands of Christ Jesus, you'll be amazed at the marvelous things He can do with you and through you. So strengthen your faith through praise, through worship, through Bible study, and through prayer. Then, trust

God's plans. Your Heavenly Father is standing at the door of your heart. If you reach out to Him in faith, He will give you peace and heal your broken spirit.

PROMISES FROM GOD'S WORD

Now faith is the reality of what is hoped for, the proof of what is not seen.

Hebrews 11:1 HCSB

For whatever is born of God overcomes the world. And this is the victory that has overcome the world— our faith.

1 John 5:4 NKJV

For we walk by faith, not by sight.

2 Corinthians 5:7 HCSB

If you do not stand firm in your faith, then you will not stand at all.

Isaiah 7:9 HCSB

A TIMELY TIP

The quality of your faith will help determine the quality of your day and the quality of your life.

—◆—✠—◆—

There are a lot of things in life that are difficult to understand. Faith allows the soul to go beyond what the eyes can see.

John Maxwell

The popular idea of faith is of a certain obstinate optimism: the hope, tenaciously held in the face of trouble, that the universe is fundamentally friendly and things may get better.

J. I. Packer

When you enroll in the "school of faith," you never know what may happen next. The life of faith presents challenges that keep you going—and keep you growing!

Warren Wiersbe

Nothing is more disastrous than to study faith, analyze faith, make noble resolves of faith, but never actually to make the leap of faith.

Vance Havner

Faith is to believe what you do not see; the reward of this faith is to see what you believe.

St. Augustine

Sometimes the very essence of faith is trusting God in the midst of things He knows good and well we cannot comprehend.

Beth Moore

A PRAYER FOR TODAY

Dear Lord, help me to be a man of faith. Help me to remember that You are always near and that You can overcome any challenge. With Your love and Your power, Lord, I can live courageously and faithfully today and every day. Amen

CHAPTER 37

THE PROMISE

If you spend quiet time with God
each day, you'll be richly rewarded.

Be still, and know that I am God . . .

—

Psalm 46:10 KJV

SPENDING QUIET TIME WITH GOD

Are you so busy that you rush through the day with scarcely a single moment for quiet contemplation and prayer? If so, it's time to reorder your priorities.

We live in a noisy world, a world filled with distractions, frustrations, and complications. But if we allow the distractions of a clamorous world to separate us from God's peace, we do ourselves a profound disservice. If we are to maintain righteous minds and compassionate hearts, we must take time each day for prayer and for meditation. We must make ourselves still in the presence of our Creator. We must quiet our minds and our hearts so that we might sense God's will, God's love, and God's Son.

Has the busy pace of life robbed you of the peace that might otherwise be yours through Jesus Christ? Nothing is more important than the time you spend with your Savior. So be still and claim the inner peace that is your spiritual birthright: the peace of Jesus Christ. It is offered freely; it has been paid for in full; it is yours for the asking. So ask. And then share.

PROMISES FROM GOD'S WORD

Be silent before Me.

Isaiah 41:1 HCSB

Be silent before the Lord and wait expectantly for Him.

Psalm 37:7 HCSB

Truly my soul silently waits for God; from Him comes my salvation.

Psalm 62:1 NKJV

But those who wait on the Lord shall renew their strength; they shall mount up with wings like eagles, they shall run and not be weary, they shall walk and not faint.

Isaiah 40:31 NKJV

My soul, wait silently for God alone, for my expectation is from Him.

Psalm 62:5 NKJV

A TIMELY TIP

Be still and listen to God. He has something important to say to you.

When we are in the presence of God, removed from distractions, we are able to hear him more clearly, and a secure environment has been established for the young and broken places in our hearts to surface.

John Eldredge

There are times when to speak is to violate the moment—when silence represents the highest respect. The word for such times is reverence.

Max Lucado

The remedy for distractions is the same now as it was in earlier and simpler times: prayer, meditation, and the cultivation of the inner life.

A. W. Tozer

Be still: pause and discover that God is God.

Charles Swindoll

Instead of waiting for the feeling, wait upon God. You can do this by growing still and quiet, then expressing in prayer what your mind knows is true about Him, even if your heart doesn't feel it at this moment.

Shirley Dobson

Be quiet enough to hear God's whisper.

Anonymous

A PRAYER FOR TODAY

Dear Lord, let me be still before You. When I am hurried or distracted, slow me down and redirect my thoughts. When I am confused, give me perspective. Keep me mindful, Father, that You are always with me. And let me sense Your presence today, tomorrow, and forever. Amen

CHAPTER 38

THE PROMISE

God will lead you along a path
of His choosing if you let Him.

Trust in the Lord with all your heart,
and do not rely on your own understanding;
think about Him in all your ways,
and He will guide you on the right paths.

—

Proverbs 3:5-6 HCSB

TRUST HIM

When our dreams come true and our plans prove successful, we find it easy to thank our Creator and easy to trust His divine providence. But in times of sorrow or hardship, we may find ourselves questioning God's plans for our lives.

On occasion, you will confront circumstances that trouble you to the very core of your soul. It is during these difficult days that you must find the wisdom and the courage to trust your Heavenly Father despite your circumstances.

Are you a man who seeks God's blessings for yourself and your family? Then trust Him. Trust Him with your relationships. Trust Him with your priorities. Follow His commandments and pray for His guidance. Trust Your Heavenly Father day by day, moment by moment—in good times and in trying times. Then, wait patiently for God's revelations . . . and prepare yourself for the abundance and peace that will most certainly be yours when you do.

PROMISES FROM GOD'S WORD

For the eyes of the Lord range throughout the earth to show Himself strong for those whose hearts are completely His.

2 Chronicles 16:9 HCSB

He granted their request because they trusted in Him.

1 Chronicles 5:20 HCSB

Let us hold fast the confession of our hope without wavering, for He who promised is faithful.

Hebrews 10:23 NKJV

The one who understands a matter finds success, and the one who trusts in the Lord will be happy.

Proverbs 16:20 HCSB

I know whom I have believed and am persuaded that He is able to guard what has been entrusted to me until that day.

2 Timothy 1:12 HCSB

A TIMELY TIP

Because God is trustworthy—and because He has made promises to you that He intends to keep—you are protected.

God is God. He knows what he is doing. When you can't trace his hand, trust his heart.

Max Lucado

Faith does not eliminate problems. Faith keeps you in a trusting relationship with God in the midst of your problems.

Henry Blackaby

Do not be afraid, then, that if you trust, or tell others to trust, the matter will end there. Trust is only the beginning and the continual foundation. When we trust Him, the Lord works, and His work is the important part of the whole matter.

Hannah Whitall Smith

Beware of trusting in yourself, and see that you trust in the Lord.

Oswald Chambers

Never be afraid to trust an unknown future to a known God.

Corrie ten Boom

The hope we have in Jesus is the anchor for the soul—something sure and steadfast, preventing drifting or giving way, lowered to the depth of God's love.

Franklin Graham

A PRAYER FOR TODAY

Dear Lord, as I take the next steps on my life's journey, let me take them with You. Whatever the coming day may bring, I will thank You for the opportunity to live abundantly. I will be Your faithful, faith-filled servant, Lord—and I will trust You—this day and forever. Amen

CHAPTER 39

THE PROMISE

God offers you a life
of spiritual abundance and peace.

I am come that they might have life,
and that they might have it more abundantly.

—

John 10:10 KJV

ACCEPTING GOD'S ABUNDANCE

The familiar words of John 10:10 should serve as a daily reminder: Christ came to this earth so that we might experience His abundance, His love, and His gift of eternal life. But Christ does not force Himself upon us; we must claim His gifts for ourselves.

Every man knows that some days are so busy and so hurried that abundance seems a distant promise. It is not. Every day, we can claim the spiritual abundance that God promises for our lives . . . and we should.

Thomas Brooks spoke for believers of every generation when he observed, "Christ is the sun, and all the watches of our lives should be set by the dial of his motion." Christ, indeed, is the ultimate Savior of mankind and the personal Savior of those who believe in Him. As His servants, we should place Him at the very center of our lives. And, every day that God gives us breath, we should share Christ's love and His abundance with a world that needs both.

PROMISES FROM GOD'S WORD

Until now you have asked for nothing in My name. Ask and you will receive, that your joy may be complete.

John 16:24 HCSB

And God is able to make every grace overflow to you, so that in every way, always having everything you need, you may excel in every good work.

2 Corinthians 9:8 HCSB

My cup runs over. Surely goodness and mercy shall follow me all the days of my life; and I will dwell in the house of the Lord forever.

Psalm 23:5-6 NKJV

And He said to them, "Take heed and beware of covetousness, for one's life does not consist in the abundance of the things he possesses."

Luke 12:15 NKJV

A TIMELY TIP

God wants to shower you with abundance—your job is to let Him.

***

Jesus intended for us to be overwhelmed by the blessings of regular days. He said it was the reason he had come: "I am come that they might have life, and that they might have it more abundantly."

Gloria Gaither

God's riches are beyond anything we could ask or even dare to imagine! If my life gets gooey and stale, I have no excuse.

Barbara Johnson

People, places, and things were never meant to give us life. God alone is the author of a fulfilling life.

Gary Smalley & John Trent

It would be wrong to have a "poverty complex," for to think ourselves paupers is to deny either the King's riches or to deny our being His children.

Catherine Marshall

The Bible says that being a Christian is not only a great way to die, but it's also the best way to live.

Bill Hybels

Jesus wants Life for us, Life with a capital L.

John Eldredge

A PRAYER FOR TODAY

Dear Lord, thank You for the joyful, abundant life that is mine through Christ Jesus. Guide me according to Your will, and help me become a man whose life is a worthy example to others. Give me courage, Lord, to claim the spiritual riches that You have promised, and show me Your plan for my life, today and forever. Amen

CHAPTER 40

THE PROMISE

God offers you the gift of eternal life
through His Son.

*For God so loved the world, that he gave his
only begotten Son, that whosoever believeth in him
should not perish, but have everlasting life.*

—

John 3:16 KJV

FOR GOD SO LOVED THE WORLD

God's grace is not earned . . . thank goodness! To earn God's love and His gift of eternal life would be far beyond the abilities of even the most righteous man or woman. Thankfully, grace is not an earthly reward for righteous behavior; it is a blessed spiritual gift which can be accepted by believers who dedicate themselves to God through Christ. When we accept Christ into our hearts, we are saved by His grace.

The familiar words of Ephesians 2:8 make God's promise perfectly clear: It is by grace we have been saved, through faith. We are saved not because of our good deeds but because of our faith in Christ.

God's grace is the ultimate gift, and we owe to Him the ultimate in thanksgiving. Let us praise the Creator for His priceless gift, and let us share the Good News with all who cross our paths. We return our Father's love by accepting His grace and by sharing His message and His love.

Have you thanked God today for blessings that are too numerous to count? Have you offered Him your heartfelt prayers and your wholehearted praise? If not, it's time slow down and offer a prayer of thanksgiving to the One who has given you life on earth and life eternal.

If you are a thoughtful Christian, you will be a thankful Christian. No matter your circumstances, you owe God so much more than you can ever repay, and you owe Him your heartfelt thanks. So thank Him . . . and keep thanking Him, today, tomorrow, and forever.

You, therefore, my child,
be strong in the grace
that is in Christ Jesus.

—

2 Timothy 2:1 HCSB

PROMISES FROM GOD'S WORD

Therefore let us approach the throne of grace with boldness, so that we may receive mercy and find grace to help us at the proper time.

Hebrews 4:16 HCSB

For the law was given through Moses; grace and truth came through Jesus Christ.

John 1:17 HCSB

Therefore, since we are receiving a kingdom that cannot be shaken, let us hold on to grace. By it, we may serve God acceptably, with reverence and awe.

Hebrews 12:28 HCSB

But God, who is abundant in mercy, because of His great love that He had for us, made us alive with the Messiah even though we were dead in trespasses. By grace you are saved!

Ephesians 2:4-5 HCSB

A TIMELY TIP

God offers you a priceless gift: the gift of eternal life. If you have not already done so, accept God's gift today—tomorrow may be too late.

———— ✠ ————

When I consider my existence beyond the grave, I am filled with confidence and gratitude because God has made an inviolable commitment to take me to heaven on the merits of Christ.

Bill Hybels

When you experience grace and are loved when you do not deserve it, you spend the rest of your life standing on tiptoes trying to reach His plan for your life out of gratitude.

Charles Stanley

While grace cannot grow more, we can grow more in it.

C. H. Spurgeon